Childhood

Childhood

BILL COSBY

Introduction by
Alvin F. Poussaint, M.D.

BERKLEY BOOKS, NEW YORK

Flexibook™

This Berkley book contains the complete
text of the original hardcover edition.

CHILDHOOD

A Berkley Book / published by arrangement with
the author

PRINTING HISTORY
G. P. Putnam's Sons edition / January 1991
Published simultaneously in Canada
Berkley trade paperback edition / November 1992

//////////////////

**My warm thanks
to Ralph Schoenstein,
whose voice once again
has blended with mine.**

//////////////////

Contents

//

////////////////

Boyhood is the meal men sup
for the rest of their lives.
—LEON URIS

////////////////

Introduction

by Alvin F. Poussaint, M.D.

*It is popular today to say that we
have to find the child within us.
For me, this would be a short search.*

—BILL COSBY

Let me take a moment to say a word or two about Bill Cosby and about his book. That Cosby has never completely grown up is surely a boon to the world. He is well acquainted with the mischievous boy within, and, more than any other comedian, has a magical rapport with children. His novel humor and his homespun anecdotes highlight the common joys and hardships in the daily lives of people like you and me.

What emerges in this volume is universal yet unique; the stories provide many stimuli for recalling the forgotten shenanigans of our own early years. Cosby grew up poor in a low-income housing project in Philadelphia, but his stories avoid the formula of humor in the face of adversity. Cosby was a devilish kid, but not a delinquent. He would be the first to recognize that in the double-edged inner-city environment, some kids make it and some don't. Despite their social drawbacks, many children and families in his neighborhood, like those in any community, were hoping and striving for opportunities to make the American Dream a reality.

Cosby's loving family and network of friends laughed, cried, fought, and played in the manner of families and neighbors everywhere. Cosby improvised games and activities, as urban and rural children do all over the world. Today, however, he casts a jaundiced eye on some of the younger generation in America who, he feels, are overly addicted to TV and high-tech electronic games and toys. "My friends and I had recreational *imagination*: We played so much more creatively than the kids play today.

"Most kids today don't use the street as an amusement park the way my friends and I did," Cosby laments. "Recreational imagination," he charges, is in short supply in today's children, whose anthem seems to be, "Mom, I'm bored." Darting between sewers and cars, he and his friends, including Fat Albert, Weird Harold, and his brother Russell, not only played stickball and street football; they improvised constantly: "The essence of childhood, of course, is play, which my friends and I did endlessly on streets that we reluctantly shared with traffic."

Cosby describes in detail many other street games, including buck-buck (known in some cities as Johnny-on-the-pony), and sporting activities centered around the fabled pink-red Spal*deen* rubber ball, which has fallen into disuse.

Cosby and his friends didn't find their fun exclusively in physical activities; they also indulged in verbal jousting. Their constant repartee included games of "the dozens"—rhyming, often profane creations in English designed to one-up an opponent psychologically. These oral fencing styles were the precursors of modern "rapping." Like that of other youngsters in difficult circumstances, the language skills of Cosby and his friends helped them survive and discover laughter in an often harsh environment. But he is not complaining: "Children today seem to need considerably more guidance than I received."

Cosby's perception that today's children are sometimes less creative than those of his day is subject to debate, but there is no argument about one characteristic that most children, past and present, share: challenging the assumptions of the adult world. Cosby describes the feigned innocence and guile that he and his friends mustered to confound and outwit grownups. Parents, relatives, and of course, schoolteachers, were prime victims of their mischief. Many children still abide by young Cosby's philosophy: "Civilization simply had too many rules for me, so I did my best to rewrite them."

The children depicted in this volume are certainly rebellious, but they also have charm, enthusiasm, and seemingly boundless creative energy. Cosby says, "Only a child can make you think that the best place for homework is in an entertainment complex." He engages in constant battles with his own children, trying to grasp the nature of their illogic.

Childhood is, experts suggest, the time we spend trying to grow and develop into logical adults. But as Cosby illustrates in this book, childhood is an experience in its own right, to be fully appreciated without needless "hurrying" along.

Cosby ends this treatise by bringing us to the stage of development that he calls "pre-pubescence." He reflects on these adolescent awakenings in an account of his group's abortive attempt to foist Spanish Fly, the mythical aphrodisiac, on a number of girls at a party.

These anecdotes about early puberty reveal how attitudes that project women as sex objects become embedded in young, hormone-driven, macho minds. Nevertheless, the early crushes of Cosby and his friends were marked by adoration, if not complete respect, for members of the opposite sex. The young fellows learned the hard way as, time and again, they got their comeuppance from the girls.

Cosby's presentation of this comedic journey through childhood to early adolescence helps us appreciate the universal language of children that bridges generation gaps and transcends time. Though Cosby chides today's couch potatoes, he concedes that the dynamic tension between generations challenges people to change and grow, making the world a more interesting and enjoyable place to be.

Above all, he convinces us that *Childhood* is never boring. As you will see, it is a perfect vehicle for his unique brand of humor as Cosby relishes "the shining simplicity and eloquent candor that could only have come from a child."

Preface

AND I CAN TAKE YOU OUT

The French like to say, "The more things change, the more they stay the same." These words do not, of course, refer to the birth of a butterfly, but they do refer to childhood, which has basically been the same ever since Cain decided he wanted to be an only child. The only difference between the childhood I lived and childhood today is that I didn't expect my parents to be social directors for me. I never once said I was bored, for children began to be bored only in June of 1963. I was a boy in a time when kids endlessly amused themselves, when a toddler exercise class was one toddler pounding another.

Today's child tells his parents, "You brought me here. Now entertain me."

If I ever had said these words to my father, he would

have smilingly replied, "Yes, I brought you here and I can take you out. I can make another one that's got to be better."

However, he didn't take me out: he let me finish childhood and then go on to get married and turn my own five children loose on an unprepared world.

It is popular today to say that we have to find the child within us. For me, this would be a short search. I am fifty-four now, but I am still the kid who put the snowball in my mother's freezer so that, one summer day, I could hit my brother with what he thought was a new ice age. I am still the kid who believed that Frankenstein lived not in Transylvania but Pennsylvania. And I am still the kid who fell so dizzily in love with a sixth-grade girl when I was a school crossing guard that I almost waved her under a bus.

No matter how old I am, these memories will always be with me, just as your own childhood is probably clearer in your mind than the place where you left your glasses. Well, you can find them later. Let's focus now on that sweet scene known as childhood.

Childhood

1

Lullaby and Good Luck

As I have discovered by examining my past, I started out as a child. Coincidentally, so did my brother. My mother didn't put all her eggs in one basket, so to speak: she gave me a younger brother named Russell, who taught me what was meant by "survival of the fittest."

I have always felt sorry for only children because they are deprived of the opportunity of being rolled out of bed by a relative. For me, the relative was Russell, with whom I was closer than I ever wanted to be. We slept in one bed in a two-bedroom apartment, where I also got close to music because my marbles kept rolling under the piano.

"Somebody's gonna kill himself on your marbles," my mother would say.

"Only somebody walkin' under the piano," I would reply, trying to show that all my marbles were accounted for.

"Well, don't come runnin' to *me* when your father falls on 'em an' then decides to fall on *you*."

"He falls okay without marbles," I said, thinking of certain Saturday nights.

To be fair to my father, the man spent many years wrestling with a question that no parent has ever been able to answer:

What's wrong with that boy?

For some reason, things that had been endearing when done by Huck Finn lost their charm when done by me. Mark Twain would have appreciated my putting a frog in my father's milk, but my father did not care for a breakfast of marine life.

"There's a *frog* in my milk," he noted one morning. "Bill, *you* know how a frog got into my milk?"

"They can really get around," I replied.

"And I wonder how *you'll* be getting around," he said meaningfully.

No matter what threat my father ever made or carried out, I loved him very much, even though he didn't understand me. He did not, for example, understand why one day I painted four butterflies on his boxer shorts. But a child today who decorated Dad's drawers would at once be enrolled in a class in abstract art, and the child's mother would be stopping strangers to say, "My Andrew is an absolute genius at underwear impressionism. He just did a jock strap that belongs in the Louvre!"

My brother Russell, however, understood me well. He understood that I had great moves in bed, where the two of us constantly fought for control of one small mattress. Night after night in the darkness of our bedroom, we were opponents in pajamas. Although I was six years older than Russell, I managed to be just as immature.

Do you know the way your children often pick bedtime for their liveliest fights? Well, Russell and I staged Philadelphia battles as memorable as Rocky's.

"This is my side of the bed," I told him one night, "and I don't want you on it."

"What do you mean your side of the bed?" said Russell. "Ain't nobody owns a side."

"Well, I do an' this is it, an' I'm tellin' you I don't want your body touching my body on my side of the bed."

"An' I'm tellin' you I'll move to any side of the bed I want: the right side, the left side, or any of the others."

"Any but my side. I don't want you touching anything, like me."

Doesn't this scene make your own children's fights seem like leaps of intellect?

"How come all of a sudden you don't want anybody touching you?" said Russell.

"For a very good reason," I told him. "Because

you are not really my brother."

He seemed surprised by this news; he had presumed we were closely related.

"Well, I'm *somebody's* brother."

"That could be. You just don't happen to be mine."

"How do you know? You look it up or somethin'?"

"Because you weren't born here."

"An' who brought me here? The *stork?*"

"No, the police. They said, 'Take care of this boy until he starts touching.' "

It was not possible for Russell and me to take to a lower level what was already the most stupid conversation in the history of sibling rivalry. Both of us, however, were eager to continue, so we now gave a new dimension to the exchange: violence.

"I can touch your raggedy old body anytime I want to," said Russell, emphasizing his point by belting me in my chest.

"You take that back!" I said.

"No, I won't; it's all yours."

"Okay then, you take *this*. And I got you last!"

"Not anymore," he said with another punch.

The bed had become a boxing ring with two feebleminded flyweights.

"Well, I'm hitting you *two* times last!" I said.

"And I'm hitting you *three* times last!" he replied.

The two of us were nicely proving that Darwin had been wrong. With nitwit dedication, we kept trying to top each other in landing the most final blows until

Russell had to stop to blow his nose because he was crying.

"Be quiet, you fool!" I said, a suggestion that made him cry even louder, until there came a voice from outside the room that I'd been expecting:

"What's going *on* in there?"

"Oh, that ain't us, Dad," I said.

"Well, you take a message to whoever it is. You tell 'em if they don't quiet down, I'm comin' in with my belt."

"I'll be happy to tell 'em, Dad, if I happen to see 'em."

And then I turned to Russell and fiercely whispered, "You don't shut up, Dad's comin' in with his belt an' it'll rip the meat off your bones. You'll wish *I* was hittin' you again."

"You hit me in the eye," he said through his whimpers, "an' my *eyeball* fell out."

"Well, if it did, I'm sorry an' I'll find it for ya. It's gotta be right here in the bed."

"You always hit people in the face."

"That's a lie: I hit Fat Albert an' I can't even reach his face. Nobody can. Look, I said I'm sorry. Now if you don't take my apology, I'm gonna bust you one."

"Sure, hit a *little* guy."

"That's the only guy in the bed."

"You hit me in the face an' I'm tellin' Dad."

"Good. Commit suicide."

"Hey, why'd you pull the covers offa me?"

" 'Cause I don't have none on this side."

"Well, don't take mine."

"Look, Russell, I'm gettin' tired of you wettin' the bed an' then I roll over in the cold spot."

"It ain't always cold."

"By the time *I* get there, it is."

"I hate you! I hate *all* brothers!"

"That includes you."

Suddenly, the bedroom door opened and my father appeared. "Okay, you two, what's goin' on in here?"

"Nothing, Dad—really *nothing*," I said, buying time for a miracle to save us, perhaps Philadelphia's first tidal wave.

"Then why is Russell crying?"

"He fell out of bed, Dad, and right on his eye. Didn't you, Russ?"

"Yeah, Dad, I think that's what happened," said Russell. "See, I was up on the bed—"

"Havin' a bad dream," I said.

"Right, havin' a bad dream. An' I fell down in the dream an' he tried to catch me an' my eye hit his fist 'cause it was my side of the bed."

"That's the most stupid story I ever heard," my father said.

Some philosopher once said, "Children and fools cannot lie." He, of course, was one of the latter. Do you want to be certain that your children are telling the truth? Then limit your questions to the names of their schools.

"It only *sounds* stupid," I said. "You gotta understand he kept sayin' they were his covers."

"But you said the police brought me and this ain't really my father."

"Now listen to me, you two. If I hear any more cryin' or arguin' or heavy breathin', I'm comin' in here with The Belt or maybe a machete. Go to *sleep!*"

"And *another* thing," said Russell after Dad had left, for the thing that best defines a child is the total inability to receive information from anything not plugged in, "get your cold feet off me, man."

"That's the temperature feet are supposed to be, you jerk," I said.

"Not *human* feet. Get 'em *off!*"

"Be quiet. Dad's at the door with a machete."

"What's that?"

"An Italian machine gun."

"Hey, you know what *I* can do?"

"I don't care, unless it's leavin' the bed and goin' to sleep on the roof."

"I can jump up and down on the bed and almost hit my head on the ceiling."

"Russell, your head ain't workin' right *now*. You wanna break it even more?"

"Wanna see me do it?"

"Sure, I never saw the inside of a head."

For the next couple of minutes, Russell put everything he had into trying to fracture his skull by using the bed as a trampoline. At least he soon would be asleep.

"I betcha we could do it *together*," he said after one of his landings. " 'Cause that's a lotta bodies, an' if we get a lotta bodies bouncin', it'll really go up."

Although Russell's grasp of physics was hardly Newtonian, I let him grab my hand as we began jumping together. Moments later, one of our landings produced a great crack that I hoped was in Russell and not in the bed; but unfortunately, he was fine.

"Oh, man," he said, "now you done it: you broke the bed!"

"*I* broke the bed?" I cried. "*You* started the jumpin'."

"But it's broke on your side."

"An' you better help me fix it or your face is gonna be broke on your side."

"I think I'd like to do a little face breaking too," said a familiar voice as the door flew open.

This time, Russell and I both ducked under the covers of the tilted bed.

"If my sons are anywhere near this broken bed," said the voice, "I'd like to know if they have any last words."

"Dad, I gotta tell ya what happened," I said, intending to do no such thing as I reappeared. "Some man came in here and just started jumpin' on the bed. He came right through the *window*."

"You really want me to believe that, don't you?"

"Dad, I could never lie to you because you're beautiful."

My father knew, however, that I could have lied to Marilyn Monroe.

"It was his side of the bed that broke, Dad," said Russell.

"Okay, here's the story," my father said. "If I have to come back in here once more, you'll both be sleeping on hospital beds."

The moment Dad left, I thought about a reconciliation with Russell, but decided against it.

"You're the most stupid brother in the history of human families," I said. "And maybe the other kind too."

"I have to go to the bathroom," he replied. "And don't take my side of the bed while I'm gone."

This was one of those times when Russell decided to use the bathroom instead of the bed, a sign that he might have been growing up. When he returned, however, he gave a different sign by spitting a mouthful of water on me.

"That's it!" I cried. "I'm gonna *kill* you now!"

"I'll do it for you," said my father, "and I'm not even gonna ask you where all that water on the bed came from."

"And I'm gonna tell ya, Dad," I said, " 'cause I think you should know. A man came in here and dumped a whole bucket of water on us."

"The same man who jumped on the bed?"

"That's the one! Dad, he's no good."

"Okay, since you boys wanna spend the night breakin' beds an' spittin' water an' greetin' people who come in the window, I'm gonna let ya get out of bed."

"Oh, good," said Russell. "We don't gotta sleep any more, Dad?"

"Right: you'll both stand here for the rest of the night. An' if I catch either of you movin', I'm gonna kill ya or do somethin' even worse. You understand?"

My father had not been gone for more than thirty seconds when Russell turned to me and said, "An' I don't want you touchin' my side of the *floor,* neither."

Many years later, when I became a father myself, I learned that insanity in children, like radio transmission, is liveliest at night. My own children—a lot of girls and a boy—have done bed bouncing for much greater distances than Russell and I did.

Their game is musical beds and it begins with the arrival of a small person in pajamas who says, "I can't sleep." She knows what she is talking about because she has been trying to go to sleep for at least six minutes, enough time to know that she has insomnia caused by fear of darkness, thunder, and the tsetse fly. Moreover, there are snakes in her bed and she would rather have a dog.

As a wise and loving parent, my wife or I now tenderly tell the child that darkness and thunder cannot harm her, and the tsetse fly is a problem only for children in Zaire. Thus reassured, she smiles and gives me a hug and says, "I sleep with you and Mommy." I would like to tell her to take a Mister Valium and go back to her room for a couple of weeks, but few parents can resist the charm of a child at night the way my father could.

Whenever one of our children made an unscheduled arrival at our bed, my wife and I had a choice: we could let the child slip between us, or one of us could move to her bed. This, in fact, is one of the biggest parental decisions you ever must make. Do you and your husband become a sandwich for the child, or does one of you stagger back to the child's room, telling her all the way that the Loch Ness monster visits only *Scottish* kids?

After twenty years of musical beds, I have learned the wisdom of remaining in my own; it is better to be the host than the guest. The lack of sleep you get with a child in your bed is of a higher quality than the lack of sleep you get in the child's. Children's beds are smaller, and a visit to one is like a night on a train with no scenery. Moreover, if the child is under three, you will probably end up on the floor—unless you like to sleep in a crib. One night, I *did* climb into a crib and even slept there for a few minutes. I didn't mind the fetal position, but I kept hitting my head on the Busy Box, and whenever I sat up, a plastic swallow flew into my mouth.

Clearly, it makes sense to absorb the child into your own bed, where there is more room and where you will learn that the things that go bump in the night are often your kids. Doctors who warn about injuries that happen in the home overlook a common one: being kicked in the kidneys by a sleeping child. My daughter Erika, for example, was so restless whenever she slept between Camille and me that we spent the night pushing her back and forth, as if we were playing beach ball.

Being fouled and losing sleep are not, of course, the only problems in having small relatives visit your bed: there is also the matter of sex. Children who drop in at night are a means of birth control that is one hundred percent effective. In fact, for years in my house, the meaning of coitus interruptus was coitus interrupted by someone other than the participants. I cannot count the number of times that I moved toward Camille in bed, only to have her say, "Not tonight; we're expecting company."

And there is also the matter of the bed-wetting child, who gives new meaning to nocturnal floating. A mother is likely to make a serious reappraisal of reproduction when she awakens not just black and blue but soggy too, the way I often awoke after having been moistened by Russell.

Parents also must consider the psychological side of things. A child who gets used to being in bed with her mother and father runs the risk of a certain maladjustment later on, especially when she is ready for college. She may even have to lie down on a psychiatrist's couch. Will she be asking the psychiatrist to join her?

*　　*　　*

My childhood should have taught me lessons for my own fatherhood, but it didn't because parenting can be learned only by people who have no children. For example, my father's inability to turn nighttime into bedtime was handed down to my wife and me, as an anthropologist could have seen early one evening when Erika was six.

"Will Erika be going to sleep tonight?" my wife casually said.

"Well, I think a little nap before dawn wouldn't do her any harm," I replied. "I know the problem, of course: she considers sleeping an elective."

"Tell me, whose turn is it to go mad?"

"I'll take it tonight. That will leave you free for something easier—like digging a new septic tank."

And so, at seven o'clock, I gently but quakingly said to Erika, "Honey, how about getting into your pajamas?"

"Any special reason?" she said.

"Yes, you're going to bed."

"But *why?*"

"Because . . . that's what children do."

"But why?"

"Because . . . because tomorrow you have a lot of playing to do."

"I'll do some of it now. Then I won't have to do so much tomorrow."

"Look, Erika, I'm not kidding. If you're not in bed by seven-thirty . . ."

"No one else is in bed by seven-thirty."

"Nonsense: millions of children are—and don't ask for names."

Although upset by her refusal to accept the concept of sleep, I was pleased by the speed of Erika's mind: she was more articulate than Russell and I had been in the days of our bedtime gymnastics.

"I want my snack first," she said.

On some evenings, she even skipped dinner so that she could delay bedtime by requesting food.

"I want you in your pajamas first. I'll bring the cookies and milk to your bed. You remember where your bed is, don't you?"

About ten minutes later, I returned with room service and found Erika redecorating her dollhouse, and now I knew that I had to do something dramatic, but my own father's physical menace was not my style with a daughter. For a moment, I considered a bribe: *Look, what will it take to get you to sleep? Are municipal bonds okay?*

What I finally did say, however, was simple and straight from the heart.

"Come on, honey," I told her. "It's time for the floating to start."

In the floating of my boyhood, my father did not always come after Russell and me: once a week, we went after him. It was usually on a Saturday night, for that was the night Russell and I got our allowance from my father, though he never knew it.

The drama began when we heard my father come home from the corner tavern. We looked at each other from opposite sides of our feathery battlefield and one of us said:

"The Giant is home."

And then we ran to the door of our room and listened to the sounds of undressing that would put us into a higher bracket. When his pants finally hit the floor with a clunk, we knew that the bank was open and the manager soon would be asleep.

Moments later, he was snoring so loudly that a passerby would have thought we had the only chain saw in the projects. This nasal racket was the signal for Russell and me to start crawling toward solvency. Slowly, with our hearts making almost as much noise as my father's nose, we advanced like commandos into his room and went through his pockets for change that we felt he wouldn't be needing again tonight. First, of course, we had taken a moment to ask ourselves if removing money from his pants was really stealing, and when we had answered that it was, we began to crawl toward the corduroy money machine.

After the withdrawal, we quickly crawled back to our beds, where Russell decided that he didn't care whose side the money was on. It could even be touching him.

"How much d'ya think we have?" he said.

"Oh, a coupla dollars," I replied, but this was just a rough guess.

We had seventeen cents.

"Let's split it now, Bill. How much is half of seventeen?"

"We each get nine," I said, taking mine.

After devoting about thirty seconds to a review of his portfolio, Russell said, "How can mine be nine when it's eight?"

"Eight, nine, it's the same thing."

"If it's the same thing, *you* take eight."

"If you think eight is less, okay."

"Man. First you steal from Dad, then you steal from me. Who's next? You gonna stick up Mom?"

"No, and here's what we better do. We each give our extra cent to Mom."

"For Mother's Day, *yeah*. She don't have to know we stole it from Dad. And then maybe she'll like us more."

"Which is good 'cause Dad's gonna like us less when he catches us."

"I hope he don't give a reward or you'll turn me in."

"I'll split it with you."

Few moments in my childhood were as lovely as that one: lying beside my little brother and planning to buy our mother's love with money we had stolen from our father. That's what it means to be a family.

2

///

A Faceful of Soup

My family was more than my father, me, and a little fountain called Russell. In a small apartment in the Richard Allen Homes of North Philadelphia, a place called "the projects," there were also my brothers Robert and James, and the head of our particular game preserve, my mother, Anna Cosby. Trains kept running past our windows and my father kept running to the saloon, but my mother was always there—except, of course, when she was out in the streets hunting for me.

I can see her now, marching down the street at nightfall to find out why her message for me to return had produced no response. At some point after I had been away from the house for more than a day or two, a message would be brought by some boy or bookie that my mother wanted me home in sixty seconds, if I still remembered the address. Unfortunately, I could not leave a stickball game that was in the seventeenth inning: I had to put my duty to sport ahead of showing my mother that I was still alive.

A few minutes later, another message arrived: If I did not come home with the speed of sound, there would be a beating and it would involve me. But now the streetlights had come on and a night game had begun, one in which we often were guessing the location of the ball. The two most fundamentally American things, Baseball and Mother, were now in dramatic opposition.

When she arrived, I was about to come to bat, but suddenly it seemed like a good idea for me to have a pinch hitter; and so, I turned and started walking about five yards ahead of her, hoping that people would think she had run into me by coincidence while going in the same direction.

The moment we reached our house, I braced myself for a spanking, but instead she took a roast beef from the oven and said, "I hope you like it well done."

"The well doner, the better," I said in relief.

"I generally don't cook it for more than ten hours."

"Hey, that's *funny,* Mom."

"Well, *you* ain't. I had to keep warmin' this up. You forget that dinner comes every night?"

"I couldn't just leave the game."

"That's what I had in mind. I was worried about

you, with those cars comin' in the dark."

"Oh, most of 'em got headlights, an' they always stop if somebody's at bat. They don't run over the hitters."

"I can't tell you how good that makes me feel. Okay, you're home an' it's time for dinner, which it's been for a while. So go in an' wash your hands."

"Sure thing, Mom," I said, and I walked to the bathroom for that cherished childhood ritual called pretending to wash your hands. First, I turned on the water and splashed it freely around the sink, the countertop, and the medicine chest (a passerby might have thought it had rained); and then I wet the soap, which was the first thing a mother checked when suspecting that her son had gone to the bathroom merely on a ceremonial visit. Finally, I carefully wet about half of a towel and crumpled it. This whole grand deception, of course, took longer than the time it would have taken me to wash my hands, but it was the principle of the thing.

When I returned to the table, my mother was looking perplexed, and I feared that she could sense the undisturbed dirt on my hands. Her question, however, concerned a different deception of mine. Holding up a quart of chocolate milk, she said, "You have any idea where this came from?"

"From the refrigerator?" I said.

"Or maybe the Easter Bunny. Since when have you been buyin' milk?"

"Well, Mom, I didn't exactly *buy* it . . ."

"You mean you sto——"

"No, no, the milkman left it."

"We don't use the milkman."

"I don't mean he left it *here*."

"Bill, there are people in prisons tellin' truer stories than this."

"Well, if ya want the truth . . ."

"I'm not sure I'd recognize it anymore."

"Russell an' I . . . y' see, we wrote a note for Mrs. Robinson across the hall an' stuck it in her empty bottle. We asked for some chocolate milk. Russell wanted a chocolate cake too, but that didn't seem right somehow. So we really didn't *steal* the milk from Mrs. Robinson."

"At least I hope your spellin' was good."

I smiled brightly. "Yeah! An' my penmanship too."

She smiled back and sighed. "How can I get angry at somebody who goes into crime to drink milk?"

In spite of our deep mutual love, my mother and I still managed to spend a lot of time embarrassing each other. She had a son who was a chocolate milk con man, and I had a mother who made citizen's arrests at stickball games. She also made me the only baseball player in Philadelphia whose uniform was a different color for every game. As a laundress, she was batting .120.

My mother had the chance to keep redesigning my uniform because I had joined a Police Athletic League baseball team when I was eleven. Although my major talent was basketball, I now found myself playing second base, and I would have been brilliant there had I been able to pick up ground balls. Nevertheless, I wore the uniform with pride. In fact, one day I wore it to school.

"William," said my teacher, "does this look like Shibe Park to you?"

"Oh, no," I replied. "This is a school."

"An excellent answer. So tell me: Why are you wearing a baseball uniform?"

"Gee, I didn't know I had it on."

"You mean you put it on by mistake?"

"Yeah, that musta been it."

And then she stared hard at me. "By the way, exactly what *color* is that uniform?"

To get the answer, I had to look down at myself, for my mother put something in her laundry that kept making the uniform a new color, or two or three; there were times I resembled the Hungarian flag.

"What team you with?" said a boy named Calvin as we were walking out of the classroom. "The Boston *Pink* Sox?"

"I'll give you a pink eye," I told him.

"Oh, he can get that himself," said a girl beside us. "*I* had it last week."

As if my motley uniform were not humiliation enough, I now knew that my threat for Calvin was something that a *girl* could get on her own! I often made them laugh at school, but always with my mouth, never my pants.

"I guess she told you," said Calvin with a mocking smile.

"Yeah, an' I'm tellin' *you*," I said: "Meet me in the schoolyard at three o'clock!"

"I'll be there."

"Well, so will I."

It seemed there was an opening in my schedule to get myself killed at three. I did, however, feel that I could beat this guy. Didn't he put on his pants one leg at a time, just as I did?

Absolutely. And after they were on, he beat the crap out of me. Not only did I lose in a flash, but I didn't even have the comfort of bleeding pitiably to win the heart of some girl; the entire fight crowd was Fat Albert.

While limping home that afternoon, I suddenly remembered my promise to my father after fearing I had hurt a boy in a boxing match: that I would retire from the ring. Of course, in a way, I *had* retired: early in the fight.

That evening, I managed to overlook one of my principles and washed my hands and face before dinner to remove the signs of the fight, and then I went to the table to fill a stomach still aching from Calvin's blows. Once again, the great presence was my mother, and once again, we were involved in the business of embarrassment.

"Are those your elbows I see on the table?" she said.

"Yep," I said, "they're mine."

"Well, how many times do I have to tell you? Keep your elbows *off* the table."

"But that's where they fit."

"I sure hope you're doin' better in school than you are learnin' manners."

"Just watch me now," I said, bending down to inhale some chicken soup.

"And that's another thing: keep your face outa the soup. Soup's gotta be brought *up;* you can't go travelin' down to it."

"Gotcha."

"An' don't talk with your mouth full o' food."

Civilization simply had too many rules for me, so I did my best to rewrite them. For example, one day early in 1945, when I was an eight-year-old student in Anna Cosby's soup eating class, I happened to learn from a girl in school that the Japanese moved their heads toward their soup, a habit that struck me as having the wisdom of the Orient.

"Momma," I said at dinner that night, "you know the Japanese?"

"Not personally," she said.

"Well, here's the big thing about 'em—besides being the enemy, when they eat soup, they *bow* to it."

She was silent for a moment, and then she said, "And that's why we gotta win the war."

"We gotta lick bad manners, right?"

"Right. Sometimes in this very house, where someone is drinkin' from the water bottle, even though glasses been invented. That isn't *you,* of course."

"Well, lemme think . . . Nope, not me."

"I just been wonderin' how come there's bread crumbs in the water."

"Well . . . Hey, don't you always tell me to cast my bread on the water?"

"*On,* not *in.*"

Perpendicular elbows must be genetic because I have been able to pass on my own to my children. At dinner one night a few years ago, I happened to notice that my eldest daughter's elbows straddled her plate like the legs of the Jolly Green Giant, while my youngest daughter's arm was lunging for the salt. The scene moved me to song:

> *Children, children, if you're able,*
> *Keep your elbows off the table;*
> *And a reach for salt that way*
> *Looks like a Magic Johnson play.*

"Mom," said my daughter Erinn through a mouthful of bread, "I think something has slipped in Dad."

"The only thing that's slipped," I said, "is your manners. I know it's fun to eat like Vikings, but it wouldn't be such a bad idea to use some of the manners that my mother and grandmother taught me. Why, I can even hear my grandmother right now telling me that my little song was bad manners because it's rude to sing at the table."

Just then, Erinn rose and launched herself toward the living room.

"Yes, Erinn," I called, "you may be excused."

I'm aware that table manners often make no sense, that eating peas with a fork, for example, is a way to recycle them to your plate, but I am driven to such elegant dumbness by something planted in me by my grandmother, who would have eaten pizza only with the proper knife; and such indoctrination lingers like a smallpox shot.

I can still see myself sitting down to one of my grandmother's meals and being pierced by her glare because I had reached the table forty-seven seconds after being called. I wonder how she would have glared at my daughters, who arrived at meals with the speed of the mail. Their lag, in fact, grew so great that I finally moved up their invitations. One day, as we were finishing lunch, I said, "Dinner is served."

"Start without me," said Evin.

Start without me. How my grandmother would have sputtered at that! She never got tired of telling me that eating should always be triggered by the hostess, who takes the meal's first bite. And if starting the main course before the hostess was a sin, then starting dessert before she did meant an instant consignment to hell; you might as well have grabbed an olive during grace. My children, of course, started dessert the moment they could find it.

Even when you remembered not to eat the meal backwards or bow to the soup or lunge for the salt or talk through your food or cut with your fork, there were still other rules that stood between you and the enjoyment of a meal. And the one calling for the use of a fork to lift vegetables was the one that must have been used by the KGB to make prisoners confess.

One memorable night, I spent several minutes trying to eat creamed spinach with a fork. There I sat, trying to fill those empty slots with spinach like someone flunking an IQ exam. At last, in desperation, I grabbed a piece of bread, soaked it in the spinach, and took a delightful bite.

"William!" cried my grandmother. "Using your bread as a mop! Have you forgotten the rule?"

Grandma, I still haven't forgotten. In fact, during a recent power blackout, I passed up a chance to use a piece of bread to get some peas on a fork, for I could hear you saying, "Even in the dark, bad manners will always be seen." Had Nero ever invited me to one of his bashes, I would have wondered if it was okay to use my fingers to pick up the grapes.

Like most other mothers, mine taught me that even more important than manners was *what* I ate. The food in my mouth through which I was not supposed to talk, the food that I was supposed to eat with elbows lost in space, was carefully selected by my mother to make me develop into a Paul Robeson. However, not only did I fail to become a Robeson, but I was lucky to have survived at all, for it turns out that she was actually poisoning me: her breakfasts of milk, bacon, and eggs should have been followed by Drano for my arteries; and she kept pushing spinach without ever knowing that too much spinach has the oxalic acid that creates kidney stones. Popeye was asking for a big urology bill.

Mothers, of course, have always meant well in handing down their time-honored ignorance to their children, for mothers have been trained by *their* mothers, like winemakers whose women teach each new generation the secret of making vinegar. It was my grandmother who told my mother that the way to stop Russell's bedwetting was to put a Philadelphia phone book under the foot of his bed: he would then be sleeping on an incline and his overactive bladder would be stilled by the altitude. The result of this folk medicine, however, was that Russell became the first boy on the block to wet the bed uphill.

"I don't know what went wrong," my mother told me the next day while washing the sheets. "Grandmothers usually know about such things. Maybe we needed the *Yellow Pages* too."

And it was my grandmother who also knew why I should go to bed earlier than every other boy, including toddlers: she told my mother, "It's the sleep before midnight that counts." I have no idea how my grandmother, like the grandmother before her, became an authority on the unconscious. She just seemed to know that any sleep you got after midnight was worthless; and so, she believed the following scientific logic:

(a) A child must have eight hours of sleep every night.

(b) Any sleep after midnight doesn't count.

(c) Therefore, the child has to go to bed at four in the afternoon.

*　　*　　*

Is it too strong to say that mothers have been lovingly lying to their children for ten thousand years? Let's just say that mothers have sincerely wanted to dispense child-rearing truths, but have overlooked the lab work. They have never done the proper testing to see if frogs will give a child warts or if eating fish will raise his IQ or if crossing his eyes will make them stay crossed. Through the ages, these maternal beliefs have been passing for wisdom in spite of no evidence at all, no evidence that spinach makes you strong and an apple a day keeps the doctor away. For years, I was knocked down with punches to my spinach-lined stomach by boys who ate mostly jelly beans; and children who have flunked even homeroom know that only one thing keeps the doctor away: he stopped making house calls thirty years ago.

If the doctor ever did come, he would tell us that mother was wrong when she said that we caught colds from running around outdoors on nasty days. We probably caught them *indoors,* where the cold virus travels best, and we may even have caught them from Grandma, who liked to kiss us while reminding us to put on our earmuffs and galoshes.

My own grandmother, however, did know that nasty weather had not been the cause of a cold.

"Bill's got a cold," my mother would tell her.

"Is he regular?" she would reply.

Her entire view of life, in fact, was through the large intestine.

"Bill broke his arm," my mother would tell her.

"Is he regular?" she would reply.

To my grandmother, irregularity caused most of the trouble in the world. She knew that the Japanese would never have attacked Pearl Harbor had they been mixing their rice with prunes.

She also felt that I was in danger of catching hives or scurvy from cats. The cats, however, were warning their grandchildren about *me,* for kittens had a short shelf life in the Cosby home.

During my boyhood, at least four kittens came into our house on their own, disproving the theory that cats are intelligent. From time to time in the morning, before I left for school, I went into the kitchen in my pajamas, sat down at the table, and suddenly felt a jolt of pain in one of my big toes, which a kitten had mistaken for his own breakfast. There was, of course, no point in those kittens eating themselves into any kind of shape. They didn't have to be fit to be run over.

The memory of those kittens was with me on the day that my daughter Ensa began her own collection of pets. She had just turned six when she brought home three caterpillars that she had found in a nearby park.

"And guess what, Daddy!" she cried. "They're going to become *butterflies!*"

"Honey," I said tenderly, "these caterpillars will become the kind of butterflies that eat my suits. It's a very special thing to have a gypsy moth for a pet."

A few months later, Ensa talked me into buying a

parakeet, whom she called Sam. At least she had moved up from the pets that the Department of Agriculture was spraying.

"Now, honey," I solemnly told her, "this is a commitment to another living thing. You will have to clean out Sam's cage and fly him and teach him to speak."

I quickly learned, however, that parakeets don't speak, they just chirp—often at the moment when all you need is the chirping of a bird to push you over the edge. I also learned that you don't fly them unless you're going Pan Am, and that children are happy to give you the opportunity to clean out the cage.

One day when I opened Sam's cage to clean it, I paused to read the newspaper on the bottom, and he shot past my hand and came to rest just inside the bedroom window. I was tempted to open it, start singing "Born Free," and let some hawk have lunch, but instead I tried to catch him with an inverted wastebasket. After many lunges at the spot where he had been a moment ago, I was wishing I had stuck with moths; and when I finally did catch him, he punched a tiny hole in my hand.

A few weeks later, my daughter Evin said it was her turn to have a pet, and I wisely chose one that didn't reproduce in my socks or perforate my skin: I bought her a couple of goldfish. Goldfish, of course, are not a lot of laughs, but there's something quietly simple about them. All you have to do is feed them, which Evin remembered to do about once a month. I won't say she wasn't attached to them, but one was dead for a couple of weeks before she happened to notice. A short time later, the other one committed suicide.

To ease her mourning, I bought her a hamster, which stirred strong feelings in my mother.

"I'm not setting foot in your house while you have that rat," she said.

"But, Mom," I said, "I'm just giving the children the wonderful chance for animal bonding that you gave me. Remember all my kittens?"

"Then there's a place in traffic for the rat?"

The rat, also known as a hamster called Ken, was the friskiest pet of all, especially at night, when he ran endlessly on an exercise wheel. I spent many hours lying awake to the sound of Ken's aerobics and damning the inventor of the wheel.

"I'm not saying that zoo work isn't wonderful fun for me," I told my wife one day after cleaning Ken's cage, "but I'd really like to see the girls sustain their attachment to a pet for a while—say as long as a week."

"The problem is," she said, "that hamsters, fish, and birds don't give anything *back*."

"I don't want anything back."

"Say, how about a cat?"

"A cat might be okay. In fact, that's exactly what the girls need: an independent pet that cleans itself and visits them once a week."

The following day, we got a kitten, a little piece of white fluff that sent nostalgic twinges through both of my big toes.

3

A Mother Always Knows, Sometimes

Like many other mothers, mine sometimes felt that even her infinite wisdom was not enough to handle a particular problem, so she brought in a free-lance sage. No one has ever discovered how mothers manage to find these sages, but they always seem to be females who could do well in professional wrestling. The one that my mother liked stood almost seven feet tall, wore white knee stockings, and hadn't smiled since 1943.

One day when I was nine or ten, my mother decided that this woman was just the person to cure my asthma; and so, I was honored by a voodoo house call. She marched into our apartment, looked at me grimly for a few seconds, and then said to my mother, "Get me a bowl of milk and a lizard."

Milk, of course, we had, but we'd forgotten to put lizard on our shopping list.

"I'm afraid we're fresh out of lizard," my mother told her.

"I'll go out and get some," my father said.

If he had not already liked to drink, this would have been an ideal time for him to start.

About twenty minutes later, he returned from a nearby pet store with a lizard.

"Now boil the milk," said this package of weirdness, and my mother went to the stove. "And now," said the weirdness when the boiling began, "drop in the lizard."

Until that moment, I never had realized how much I had liked having asthma.

If you're ever in the mood to launch a lizard, an excellent way is to drop one into boiling milk. When our lizard hit the milk, he shot up in the air like a little green rocket and landed not far from where I was cringing.

While my mother and father began to yell at each other, an exchange that makes sense when lizards are flying, the woman commanded us to retrieve the lizard, which was under a chair, dreaming no doubt of the relative peace of crocodile country.

With the milk still boiling (and my father too), the woman threw the lizard back in. This time, however, it did not eject: instead, it died—from scalding, drowning, or disgust. Removing the pot from the stove, she now turned to me and said, "Young man, drink this."

And my asthma was cured. In fact, just one look at that pot could have taken care of bronchitis and beriberi too.

This wildlife cure for asthma was just one of the many miraculous home remedies concocted by the medicine women who haunted the projects. If an amphibian milk shake was not to your taste, then perhaps you might have liked the cure for chicken pox, which was to smear oatmeal all over your body. Most people foolishly think that oatmeal's greatest value comes when taken internally; and there are those, of course, who do swallow it. However, when I was a boy, oatmeal smeared all over your skin became a kind of lumpy penicillin for those medicine women, who must have thought that the Mayo Clinic was a source of salad dressing.

As Louis Pasteur and Jonas Salk knew, oatmeal might have been right for chicken pox, especially if you got chicken pox at breakfast, but for chest congestion the ideal thing was a spoonful of turpentine with sugar. Even if you preferred your turpentine without sugar, that precise blend was necessary to clear your chest, and also to remove any paint that might have been in your esophagus.

One memorable afternoon in that medieval time, Russell came home with blood on the knee that I never wanted touching me. As I saw the blood oozing through his pants, I didn't consider calling a parent, a doctor, or the voodoo queen: I suddenly saw my chance to play the hero in a Western movie, for no one was home—both in the house and my head. At this moment, Russell no longer was a crying boy of six but a crying cowboy who'd been shot in a bunkhouse argument over whether a curveball broke sideways or down; and I no longer was a scrawny boy of twelve but the bravest doctor west of the Rio Grande and a genius with gunshot wounds to the knee.

Tearing apart the leg of Russell's pants, just as the doctors in Deadwood did, I saw a gash of more than an inch. At once, I knew what to do: put him in the bathtub.

"Why you puttin' me in here?" he said, not without logic as he stopped crying.

"Just trust me," I said, giving him the worst advice of his life. "Ol' Doc Cosby's gonna fix you up, pardner."

And then I put a wad of toilet paper on the wound and turned on the water. I had, however, missed the class at Frontier Medical School that told how to waterproof toilet paper. The bandage floated away.

Letting out the water, I decided to paint the wound with iodine, but I couldn't find any—and then I remembered my father's Four Roses, which had eased his pain on many a night.

"Pardner," I said, "you wait right here. I'm a-gonna give ya a lil' somethin' for yer busted hide. And while I'm a-gettin' it, I want ya t' start a-singin' a campfire song."

"Okay," he said, and he started singing,

Wontcha tell me, dear
The size of your brassiere.
Thirty—

"No, a *different* campfire song—like 'You Are My Sunshine.' An' I'll be right back."

Never was boyhood imagination in higher flight than when I went for my father's Four Roses while Cowboy Russell sat in a bathtub, oozing blood and singing,

You are my sunshine,
My only sunshine.
You make me happy
When skies are gray.

When I returned, aware that Dad's disinfectant would sting Cowboy Russell, I made him take a shot of it first, the way that wounded men were anesthetized in the Old West. And the moment he swallowed it, I made medical history, for I became the first doctor who ever had his patient drink the disinfectant too.

A few seconds later, I soaked a washcloth with Four Roses and applied it to his knee.

"Ow!" he cried. "That hurts!"

"Here, have some more painkiller," I said.

This time, I didn't give him a swallow but soaked a second washcloth with Four Roses and put it in his mouth, leaving him wincing at both ends.

"Jes' keep a-chewin' on that," I said. "You don' want nobody 'round the bunkhouse t' hear ya screamin'."

Pulling the washcloth out of his mouth, he cried, "I *hate* this stuff! I want chocolate milk!"

"Sorry, pardner: rustlers got all the chocolate milk at Dodge City. You jes' keep a-singin' while I look at that knee."

"I hate the song too. I wanna sing, 'Is You Is or Is You Ain't My Baby?'"

Removing the other washcloth, I saw that blood still oozed from the gash, so I poured some Four Roses directly on it. Russell now was smelling like an outpatient in a saloon.

"Pardner, 'fraid I gotta quarterize that."

"You gotta *what?*"

"Ya jes' hafta be brave a lil' longer. Here, take another sip."

I managed to give him some more anesthetic, which seemed to relax him. I didn't know how much whiskey was needed to make an eight-year-old drunk, but he was nicely on his way. While he began to sing a new song, I brought my mother's curling iron to the bathroom and plugged it in. The sight of the iron getting hot moved Russell to sober up at once.

"You gonna *brand* me with that thing?" he said, wondering how far into the Old West his lunatic brother would be going.

"Well, pardner, I jes' gotta—"

"First, you stick it up your ass! Go quarterize *that!*"

Deciding to respect his rights as a patient, I turned

off the iron and said, "Okay, then we gotta sew it up. That won't hurt hardly none. You jes' keep a-singin'; I'll be right back."

And from the tub there came:

Is you is or is you ain't my baby?
The way you're actin' lately makes me doubt.

The way that *I* was acting lately would have made anybody doubt, but children pretended with a frenzy in those pre-Nintendo days.

About a minute later, I returned with my mother's sewing needle, which held a long piece of white thread, and I bent down to examine Russell's ninety-proof knee. However, it suddenly seemed to me that if I stitched up the wound, I would make some new holes; and so I wrapped the knee in toilet paper and tied a piece of string around it, the kind of bandage that must have been popular in the War of the Roses.

"I've saved your knee, pardner," I said as I led him from the tub to his room. "You'll live to kick me again."

And then I helped him put on his pajamas and he got into bed, partly on my side, but I didn't mind because he'd been shot.

"How 'bout another song o' the range?" I said.

"Okay," he replied, and he sang,

My Momma done tol' me
When I was in knee pants,
My Momma—

"Oh, man!" he cried. "Momma's gonna see my pants got no *knee*. How we gonna explain that, Doctor?"

"Don't worry," I said, wondering how we also would explain why his bed smelled like a distillery. "I'll think of somethin'."

And I *would* think of something. A boy in those days always did.

Throughout my boyhood, I was under constant pressure to think of something that had a chance of being believed by my mother or father.

"How'd you get that lump on your forehead?" my mother once said when I entered the house.

"Oh, that?" I said. "I didn't notice it."

"You don't notice when the sun goes down. What hit you there?"

"Well, if you really want to know . . ."

"No, I'm askin' 'cause I don't wanna know."

"I got hit by a piece of coal."

"Bill Cosby, you've told me a lot of stories . . ."

"It's *true*: I got hit by flyin' coal."

"You was lyin' in a bin?"

"No, we was down at Thirtieth Street. The yards."

"Doin' what?"

"Playin' with trains."

"Nobody plays with *those* trains. And nobody plays with coal. You could've lost an eye instead of just losin' your brains."

"Most of it missed me."

"Bill, I want you to stop runnin' around with Junior

Barnes an' those other hoodlums an' find some new friends."

The following day on the street, during a lull in the conversation, I said as tactfully as I could to my social circle, "Listen, my mom wants me to find some new friends. You guys know any?"

"Naw," said Junior, "there ain't been any new friends around here in years. What's wrong with us?"

"She says you're hoodlums."

"I mean, what *else?*"

I felt like a hoodlum myself one day when I was boxing with Jody Cooper at Eddie Robinson's house and Jody suddenly fell down and didn't move.

"He's dead, Cos," said Weird Harold. "His mother's really gonna be sore."

"You killed him," said Fat Albert. "Hey, you gonna get the electric chair, Cos?"

"I never knew anybody that got the electric chair," said Junior. "Can I have your sneakers?"

"Well, I hope you *don't* get the electric chair," said Harold with a rush of feeling. "Then we'd be short a guard."

With Jody still motionless on the floor and my friends conducting a memorial service for both him and me, I turned and ran home.

"What's the matter with you?" said my mother, lyrics she knew well.

"Matter?" I said with all the cleverness at my command.

"Bill, I'm lookin' at you, but you're not lookin' at me."

"Well . . . it's good to exercise the eyes. Most people don't get enough, you know."

"I'm gettin' enough of *you*. Just tell me why the police are after you."

What a lucky guess.

"Mom, what makes you think somethin' like that?"

"Then what are you doin' home so early?"

"I just got tired of foolin' around."

"No you didn't 'cause that's what you're doin' with me. If you keep lyin' to me, I'm not comin' to your trial."

"Mom, I tell you, there's nothin' wrong."

"I had children, that's what's wrong. Okay, go to your room an' think about what Jesus said about lyin' to your mother."

"He was against it, right?"

"And when the police come, I'll tell 'em you're packin' for jail."

And so I went to my room. Like every naughty child since Cain, I *liked* to go to my room and never understood a punishment that sent me there. Mothers have always had this one backwards: the punishment should be, "Okay, go to the hall closet. I'm renting your room."

About an hour later, I went downstairs for dinner, where my father said, "Your mother tells me you don't look right. That's not news, of course, but she says she thinks you did something that could mean jail. Well,

I just want you to know: even though you can't go to jail at nine, I'll promise the police to watch you till you're old enough to arrest."

"Dad, I haven't done anything," I said.

"Whose house were you playin' at?"

"Nobody's in particular."

"The rent was paid by nobody in particular?"

"Well, it might have been Eddie Robinson's."

And before I could say, *Or it might have been Sugar Ray Robinson's,* my father was on his way there. I prayed that the body would be gone by the time he arrived.

He was barely out of the door when my mother said, "You burned down Eddie Robinson's house?"

"I wish it was as simple as that," I said. "See, we were boxing an' I hit Jody Cooper in the head an' . . . well, I think he's pretty unconscious right now."

"An' you'll be joinin' him. Wait till your father gets home."

"That's just the thing, Mom. Would you mind hiding me from him—just for a year or two?"

"I don't hide criminals. Whoever taught you to be a thug?"

"Maybe I could be another Joe Louis."

"You're not gonna live that long. I figure you got about another forty minutes. Anything special you wanna do with it?"

"Yes, I'd like to travel to—"

"Just wait till your father gets home."

This was one of the two great maternal pronouncements of my youth. The first was *Go to your room,* the unintentional favor that your mother did for you when she was bungling your punishment; and the other was *Wait till your father gets home*. I was lucky that mine often didn't make it.

When my father finally came back, he was laughing. I was relieved to see that he didn't care that much about Jody's death.

"Hey, Dad," I said. "Glad to see you feeling so good."

"Jody will live," he said, "and so will you if you announce your retirement from the ring right now."

"I'm hangin' up my gloves this second."

"Good. Let's keep all the hitting in this family to me hitting you. God wants it that way."

4

//

And Carry
a Small Stick

Now that I've had children of my own, I can understand the heartbreaking problem that my father had in trying to turn me into a human being. The traditional picture of the American father is a man to whom a desperate mother can turn and say, "*Do* something with this child!" And there may even be fathers who *can*, but I've never met one. To a plea of "*Do* something with this child!" the average father wants to reply, "Okay, I'll teach him how to park."

Discipline is the last thing that a father wants to consider because he doesn't like taking on tasks for which he has no talent. His only comfort is that no one else has any talent either: it is a game without seeded players. In fact, the great unspoken truth about child raising is that, in spite of the seven thousand books of expert advice, the right way to discipline a child is still a mystery to most fathers, and to most mothers too. Only your grandmother and Genghis Khan knew how to do it.

If you want to discipline a child, instead of doing something simple like training killer bees, you will find that many things are against you, one of which is the child. In comparing notes with other defeated fathers, I have gained an insight into our never having the slightest idea of what we're doing.

First of all, we fathers have learned that the advice of experts is lovely on the "Oprah Winfrey Show," but less impressive when a child is trying to restructure your shin. Some magazine once published a list of things to remember when you're trapped in quicksand. However, people trapped in quicksand always seem to forget the list and must settle for frantic improvisation, which also happens to be the most sensible way to discipline a child.

And even if you do manage to remember the wise advice, you will find that it loses something in the trip from the page to the tantrum. For example, psychologists often suggest that a parent reason with a child during a fit—the fit of the child, that is, not the parent. *Ask him why he did it,* says one prominent psychologist. Well, one day I decided to try an adventure in rationality with one of my girls by softly inquiring, "Honey, why did you step on your sister's face?"

"Because I hate her guts," she replied.

"And I can respect that, as a momentary feeling, of course. But the next time you're so moved, why not talk to her about it instead of trying to break her jaw, which affects *her* side of the dialogue."

"Daddy, how can I talk to people I hate?"

She had made an interesting philosophical point, and one of these days, I may come up with a reply. But replies are dangerous, as I learned a few days ago when I heard this exchange between a father across the street and his five-year-old:

BOY: I want my lunch.

FATHER: Well, how do you *ask* for it?

BOY: Like this: *I want my lunch.*

The father's mistake had been in choosing the wrong time for a lesson in manners. A better time would have been the week of the boy's graduation from law school. This father did, of course, have the option of responding with toughness, but I have found that fathers generally prefer to reduce armed confrontation to peaceful diplomacy; and then we reduce peaceful diplomacy to intelligent appeasement.

Two days after this luncheon scene, I happened to be talking to another father in his driveway when his six-year-old son began to take a walk on the top of his car, perhaps with the thought of antiquing it.

"George!" cried the father. "You get down from there!"

"In a few minutes," George replied.

"I mean it: you get down right *now!*"

"No, no, no, no, no!"

"Look," the father said, "I certainly support your right to another point of view. I believe in the First Amendment. And with that in mind, get *down!*"

At last, the father underscored one of his points by pulling the boy off the car. You may be thinking that he wasted too much time on pacifism, but I have seen the hard line fail just as often and leave the father in an even weaker position. One day, a friend of mine down the street said to his eight-year-old son, "Sam, you do that again and I'll tear off your arm and beat you senseless with it!"

Sam responded by laughing, for he knew that this threat made more sense coming from a grizzly bear than his father. Laughter, of course, is not the ideal climate for a disciplinarian, especially when the disciplinarian is doing the laughing. My daughters, for example, have always known that whenever I scolded them, I was miscast and could easily be bumped from my role.

"Young lady," I sternly said to my daughter of nine one night, "I never want to see you doing that again."

"Then don't look," she said, and we both laughed. No student of children, from Dr. Freud to Dr. Seuss, has ever been able to solve this ultimate challenge: How do you handle the child who first breaks up the living room and then you?

To be fair, my father and I did share many moments besides the ones in which he tried to figure out what to do with me; and perhaps the most memorable of these took place at a movie house in our neighborhood called the Booker.

One day, my friends and I were startled by a sign in front of the Booker:

COMING SATURDAY

FRANKENSTEIN

WOLF MAN

AND

DRACULA

Unable to believe that this unholy trinity would be coming to us, we went to the theater's manager and Junior Barnes said, "Is this the *real* Frankenstein who's comin'?"

"Yes," said the manager, "and the real Dracula and Wolf Man too. Saturday midnight, all in person."

"Dracula's gonna drink blood right here?" said Eddie.

"Yes, he'll probably want a little refreshment," said the manager with a smile. "A little hemoglobin cocktail after his long trip from Transylvania."

"Is that near Camden?" I said.

An hour later, I was telling my father, "*Please,* Dad, I wanna see Frankenstein at the Booker."

"Now why would Frankenstein come to Philadelphia?" he said. "Unless he's gonna play for the Phils. Come to think of it, he moves like those boys."

"Dad, believe me, he's comin'."

"Nobody in the projects thinks he's comin'."

"They all think Jesus came."

"But not to Philadelphia. The closest thing to Frankenstein in Philadelphia is your uncle."

In spite of my father's doubts, I finally persuaded him to take me to the Booker on the big night of fright. Although my hero was Herb McKenley, the great Jamaican quarter miler, Frankenstein meant more at midnight, especially this one: Halloween.

And so, at eleven-thirty that night, I was standing in line at the Booker with my father, whose mood fell just short of being festive.

"That Frankenstein better come an' be worth fifty cents," he said.

He was, in fact, paying a dollar—that is, if he planned to take me in too.

"An' it better not be a *movie* of Frankenstein either or I'm gonna drink *your* blood."

"That ain't Frankenstein, that's Dracula," I said. "He's comin' too!"

A few minutes later, near midnight, my father and I were seated in the sixth or seventh row as the lights went down and eerie music began to play. Suddenly, the theater fell silent, while two people in the first row got up and left, clearly too frightened to take any more. I, however, was even more frightened than they because I had terror on both sides: if Frankenstein didn't get me, my father was an alternate, especially if Frankenstein didn't get me and the whole monster rally turned out to be just a Halloween trick.

And then it happened: through the curtain came a long, black-coated arm that could have belonged only to Frankenstein or a gangly headwaiter. A few women screamed and one near me fainted. Her male companion would have revived her had he not been busy running up the aisle.

With a soul-chilling sweep, the curtains now opened and there he stood: in his ill-fitting tuxedo, his orthopedic shoes, and the little hatracks on the sides of his neck. His arms were thrust straight forward, as if he wanted to come down and kill a few of his fans.

At this point, people in the front rows, some of them men, began to leave; and to avoid clogging the aisles, they used the backs of the seats as a route to the rear. Other people, however, decided it was more sensible just to stay where they were and scream.

The response to Frankenstein was lively enough, but suddenly a spotlight hit the left front corner of the theater and through an exit door came a man who needed a haircut on every part of his body.

Wolf Man!

Several more people took this opportunity to either faint or run up the aisle, while the screaming continued. And then, as if all of this were not fun enough, another yank of the curtains revealed Dracula, looking for a shot of Type A.

"Oh Jesus Christ, oh Jesus Christ," said my father, wishing he had brought a crucifix instead of me.

Although I could hear the pandemonium, I no

longer could see it because my head was buried in my father's sleeve.

"You're facin' the wrong way," he said.

"No, I'm not," I replied, addressing his elbow. "They're gonna eat me. They like to eat kids."

"Don't be stupid; they already had their dinner."

"Probably someone I know."

"Just sit up now. There's nothin' to worry about."

"Then why was you sayin' 'Jesus Christ'?"

"Don't mean nothin'. I say it at ballgames too."

"Then let's go to a ballgame."

"Look, Bill, this was your idea, so sit up and *watch*. I didn't pay a dollar for you to hide in me."

During this discussion, people were continuing to run to the rear. You may be wondering how adults were naive enough to believe that Frankenstein, Dracula, and Wolf Man were playing the Booker (dead in concert, one might say), but this was a time of wondrous innocence in America, before people knew that Martians don't visit New Jersey and Popeye had kidney stones.

In the front row of the Booker on that memorable night were three men who seemed to have no interest in going berserk: they just sat and stared at the monsters—until, that is, Frankenstein suddenly stepped down from the stage and moved toward them, followed by a growling Wolf Man. The monsters were trying to have a little ghoulish fun with the audience, but unfortunately, they hadn't chosen the three most laid-back men in the house. Within seconds, one of them jumped up and hit Frankenstein in the face, one of them chased Dracula through the curtains, and one of them took care of Wolf Man. It turned out that a silver bullet wasn't needed to take care of Wolf Man: a punch in the mouth was enough.

Today, forty-five years later, as I look back at my little face buried in my suddenly devout father, I see just how deeply we believed in fantasy when I was a boy. We believed so much in those happy days, the days before children knew that centerfielders liked sex and Batman was a manic-depressive.

5

///

Are You Majoring in Detention?

ne evening a few years ago, I was sitting at the kitchen table with my youngest child, a girl of twelve, and I was trying to do the same math homework that had stumped me in 1946.

"I'm sorry, sweetie," I said, "but I had trouble with negative numbers when *I* went to school. Zero was as low as I could go."

And then I found myself starting to sing,

The boys all called him Johnny Zero.
In school they always used to say,
"Johnny got a zero, Johnny got a zero . . ."

"You had a *song* about getting a zero?" my daughter said.

"Well, the *last* Zero Johnny got was a Japanese plane. Shot it down."

"Why was he shooting at the Japanese?"

"World War Two; we did a lot of it then."

"Did you have any teacher as rotten as Mrs. Pacelli?"

"Honey, I had teachers who make Mrs. Pacelli look like Mother Teresa."

"Who's she?"

"A nun who won the Nobel Prize for doing good things."

"Is the Nobel Prize better than a Grammy?"

I laughed. "Well, there's no video with it, but you do get a lot of money and a trip to Sweden."

"Where's that?"

"Come on, I'll show you on a map," I said, hoping she wouldn't ask what a map was.

And so, as the Lone Ranger's announcer used to say, Return with me again to those thrilling days of yesteryear, when children knew that the capital of Bolivia was not Little Rock, and that Bolivia was not a suburb of Detroit. From out of the past come the thundering footsteps of the vice-principal as he heads for the smoke signals coming from the boys' bathroom . . .

One morning, some of that smoke was coming from me. A few minutes earlier, I had been in a shop class, where once again I was displaying an inability to use my hands for anything besides scratching myself. This day's shop class, however, should have been an easy one for me. We were making ash trays and that was my style: everything I made turned out to be an ash tray.

On this particular morning, when I was *supposed* to be making an ash tray (and was probably making a door), I suddenly felt moved to see if I could also make some ashes to go with it. Coincidentally, three of my friends were similarly moved, so all of us asked the teacher for permission to go to the bathroom. Any suspicion he might have had about four synchronized bladders was outweighed by his delight at the thought of not seeing us for a while.

"Go ahead, but stay out of trouble," he said, forgetting that trouble was the only reason boys ever went to the bathroom at school.

When we got there, one of the boys lit a cigarette, inhaled a long puff, and said, "Okay, catch this. Now I'm talkin', but you don't see any smoke comin' out of my mouth, right?"

"Hey," I said, "how do you *do* that?"

"I don't use the same lungs for talkin' that I use for smokin'."

"Lemme try it."

Feeling as cool as Miles Davis, I took a deep puff, sucked in the smoke, and began to cough.

"My lungs . . . they don't want it in there."

"Which lungs you usin'?"

"These," I said, pointing to my chest.

"That's the wrong ones."

I was pondering this anatomy lesson when the bathroom door opened and the vice-principal came in. Only a second before his entry, I had tossed my cigarette into a toilet, perhaps because I didn't smoke.

"All right," he said, "who's smoking in here?"

"Not me," I quickly replied, while the other guys were wondering who they hated more: the vice-principal or me. "There was smoke in here when I came in an' I had to breathe it. Must be a short circuit in one of the toilets."

"Cosby, the short circuit is in your brain. Tell me something: What do you want to be when you grow up?"

"Quarter-mile champion! Like Herb McKenley!"

"You think *he* smokes?"

"Around the track, he sure does."

The other boys laughed.

"Well, I can tell you one thing you're *not* going to be and that's a comedian. Now all you big shots, get back to class. And *you* . . . take those toothpicks out of your mouth."

"It's a shop class," said the boy, "an' I may need some wood."

"Wise guys, the four of you. You'll end up making *license* plates in shop."

Whenever I think about those days, I'm amazed that I developed the passion for education I have, for many of the boys considered school an annoying interruption between birth and a career of stealing cars. They were such an irrepressible bunch. For example, one day, to enliven the metal shop class, Junior Barnes put a bullet in the furnace. It was not the kind of .22 we had put on the trolley tracks, but a .45, a caliber that reflected our growth. Because most of us knew that the bullet was in the furnace, we were paying even less attention to the teacher than usual. And, of course, we carefully avoided standing on the firing line, which the teacher still thought was just a furnace.

Bang!

"What the hell was that?" the teacher inquired.

"Musta been a short circuit in there," I said, giving the explanation that seemed to cover a variety of unusual phenomena in the school.

"Did one of you boys put a firecracker in there?"

"Oh, no," said a chorus of co-conspirators.

"Well, whoever did, this kind of behavior reflects on his mother."

And Junior whispered fiercely to me, "My mother never put no bullets in the stove!"

His mother, however, was a possible contributor to Junior's IQ, and *that* might have been 45.

In spite of such extracurricular activities as the testing of cigarettes and explosives, I was a good boy at the Mary Channing Wister Elementary School. In fact, when each term began, I neatly covered all my books not with plain brown paper but with brightly colored oilcloth, for there was more prestige in covering your books than reading them.

"My Bill has such beautifully covered books," my mother told a friend one day.

"I guess he's just a natural bookmaker," the friend replied.

Covering my books made me proud, but I was even prouder to be a crossing guard, to stand at the corner near the school in a sash that said SAFETY PATROL and tell kids when they could cross the street.

"You can go now," I said one day with a gracious but commanding sweep of my arm.

"We was gonna go anyway," said a small boy.

"That's what the green light means," said his friend.

"*I* know that," I said, reminding them of my qualification to be a crossing guard.

When I was eleven, my job as a crossing guard gave me my first taste of romance: whenever a certain fetching female named Elaine reached the corner, I took personal charge of her trip.

"You may go now," I told her one morning with a debonair smile and a sweep of my arm.

"But the light is red," she said.

"And so it is."

I had been too blinded by Elaine to see anything else.

"I could have gotten killed," she said.

And so she could, but she would have died for love.

In my last year at Mary Channing Wister, I became captain of the safety patrol; and now I not only dispensed dopey travel tips but I also checked on other guards to make sure that they hadn't gone to sleep or deserted.

"Harold, is this your post?" I said one day.

"Yeah, I think so," he replied.

"What're ya supposed to be doin'?"

"Watchin' for fires an' stuff."

"Anything on fire right now?"

"I don't think so. But I was in the bathroom a few minutes."

"Good. Carry on."

I had been made captain of the patrol in a ceremony at a school assembly, one of those assemblies in which the kids sang,

> *Come Thou, Almighty King.*
> *Help us Thy Name to sing.*
> *Help us to pray.*
> *Father all glorious,*
> *All or victorious,*
> *Come and reign over us . . .*

I had never understood this constant request for rotten weather. Why did we keep asking God to rain over us, especially when there were no farmers in North Philadelphia? I had no time, however, to think of farmers during the week that I worked to memorize my acceptance speech, the heart of which was *I accept.*

At last, when the big moment came and the principal turned to me, my mind went blank. Here was my first chance to perform in public and I couldn't even remember why I was up on the stage. To get an attendance award? To be graduated? To meet Frankenstein?

With a smile that made me want to strangle him,

the principal just stood there. Either he wanted me to learn self-reliance or he also had forgotten why I was there.

"I want to . . . thank you for . . . for this . . . this . . . great honor," I finally said, taking a guess.

When the assembly was over, the vice-principal gave me another bit of guidance for my life.

"Cosby," he said, "forget about ever speaking in public."

In spite of the vice-principal knowing that I would be neither a comedian nor a public speaker, and in spite of my shop teacher feeling I'd be lucky to last in an ash tray factory, I did learn more in that school than just the meanings of traffic lights. An American public school in the forties taught such classical disciplines as the ability to write a complete English sentence, the ability to tell Beethoven from the Ink Spots, and the ability to find Asia on a map. In fact, geography class made me develop so much interest in foreign lands that I even did independent study in *National Geographic,* which was a kind of *Playboy* for environmentalists.

"You better not let your mother catch you lookin' at those," said Harold one day at the start of geography class.

"Why?" I said. "She's seen those before."

"I wonder why there's so many breasts in Africa."

"Probably just as many in Philadelphia. We gotta find the right magazine."

"William!" said a stern voice from the front of the room. "What are you reading instead of your book?"

"Oh, *National Geography,* Miss Baker," I brightly replied, holding up the magazine.

"Good for you. And what particular part of the *National Geographic*—you got the name almost right— has you interested today?"

"Africa," I said uneasily.

"Especially African jugs," whispered Junior.

"Jugs?" said Miss Baker. "You like pottery, William?"

"Yeah, pots—an' pans too."

The class laughed and Miss Baker frowned.

"There is no need to make fun of a simple mistake," she said.

Simple mistake, of course, also described Junior, who had put me in this spot.

"William, pans aren't pottery. However, because of the extra reading that you've been resourceful enough to do, you may erase the blackboard and clean the erasers for class tomorrow."

"Thank you, Miss Baker," I said.

"Jesus," said Junior, "you look at some jugs an' you get the blackboard job. *I* already seen enough of 'em to make me *principal.*"

Like most kids today, my school friends and I majored in one timeless subject: writing notes. And the notes were sometimes declarations of love, which one day in a music class led to a declaration of war. While we were listening to the *Unfinished Symphony,* Harold used his unfinished brain to write to a girl nearby:

I dig you the most Sinthia. Will
you be my woman.

Cynthia wouldn't be anyone's woman for another nine years, but her callousness wasn't the problem for Harold. His problem was that his wingéd words were intercepted by Eddie, who took a moment to laugh, and then wrote back to Harold:

I dig you the most Harold honie. Will
you be my man Charlie Chan. Whats your
issue toylit tissue.

To Harold, this reply was junk mail. When he received it, he decided to get back in touch with Eddie by using a flying eraser; and then, when he had Eddie's attention, he pressed his fist against his stomach and turned it back and forth, an action that in our neighborhood was not the Heimlich maneuver. Moments later, he sent a note to Eddie that said:

Your mother puts out for sailors.

Harold, of course, was guessing about whether Eddie's mother had been involved in such naval maneuvers, a guess that seemed to bother Eddie, who now began another note. Meanwhile, other mail was going through, and much of it was profound insight into the human condition, such as:

Donna told Albert he's too fat at the Booker.

Albert was too fat at other places as well, but at the Booker he had become the subject of a class note. And now, Harold was Eddie's subject again:

> *I dont feetur that stuff about my*
> *mother. How about I beat the crap out*
> *of you. 3 oclock stairway 4 you*
> *bastid. Please anser.*

In those old-fashioned days, school fights often were made by written invitation, and the fights themselves were governed by one unwritten rule.

"Remember these are my only pants," said Harold to Eddie at three that day, "so don't mess 'em up."

"I'm just gonna mess *you* up," said Eddie thoughtfully.

In spite of this promise, I still worried more about Harold's clothes than his skin, for skin would grow back, but in the projects clothes were harder to replace. Luckily for Harold, however, the fight didn't last long enough to affect his wardrobe. Eddie, whose hobby was opening Coke bottles with his teeth, deposited Harold on the ground almost at once and then grabbed his throat.

"You take it back about my mother puttin' out for sailors!"

"Okay . . . okay," said Harold. "Not for *sailors*."

The American school has changed dramatically since those lively days of my boyhood, and the change seems to have made it a much less eventful place. In fact, nothing ever happens there now. I know this re-markable truth because every day that I met one of my children after school, I said, "How was school today?"

And the child would reply, "Okay, I guess."

"You guess? Don't you remember? It wasn't that long ago."

"Okay, I guess."

"You're still guessing. You don't have to study for these questions, you know."

"What questions?"

"Look, you just spent six hours in school. Didn't *anything* happen there today?"

"Like what?"

"Oh . . . I don't know. The arrival of locusts?"

"What're they?"

"You remember the plagues that hit Egypt?"

"Who's Egypt?"

"All right, just tell me this and then your lawyer can release you: Did everything go well in all your classes?"

"It was okay."

"And you're not guessing, right?"

I have never met a father or mother who got anything other than true-false answers to after-school questions. There is probably no way to get an essay answer, even if you asked the two questions most relevant to your child's life at school:

—Did you find any of the jackets, shoes, books, and underpants you've lost?

—Did you make any new friends in detention?

*   *   *

The best that a parent can do today is be semi-involved in the schoolwork of a child.

"Sign this test, Dad," said my youngest daughter one evening, her left hand casually draped across the top two inches of the front page.

"May I see the mark first?" I replied.

"It's not important. You and Mom always say it's learning, not marks, that counts."

"Right, and I'd like to learn about your mark."

"Trust me, I got one."

"I appreciate your sharing that with me. And now I'd like to see it."

"You mean you'll only sign for a high one? I thought you were an equal-opportunity father."

"Is it lower than a D?"

"Dad, you have to remember that a mark is merely the teacher's opinion."

"Is it lower than an F? Have you gotten the world's first G?"

"The thing is, she should have marked this test on a curve."

"I don't care if she should have marked it on a *ramp*. If you don't move your hand, I don't move mine."

Slowly, she lifted her hand to reveal a bright, red D.

"But this doesn't mean what you think," she said.

"Oh," I said, "it stands for delightful?"

"No, it's a *high* D."

"Good. You'll have no trouble getting into a barber college. Tell me, did you study for this test?"

"Oh, absolutely. I really did."

"Then how could you have gotten a D?"

"Because I studied the wrong things. But Dad, isn't it better to study the wrong things than not to study the right ones?"

And one of the wrong things to study is a child, for only a child can make you think that F is her teacher's initial.

And only a child can make you think that the best place for homework is an entertainment complex.

Perhaps the basic problem that children have today is not their concentration span, which is roughly as long as the life of a smoke ring, but their stereophonic approach to studying.

One afternoon last year, I found one of my daughters doing her homework to the accompaniment of Oprah Winfrey, who was probing a question that had confounded Socrates: Why Do Women Marry Jerks?

"You're doing a report on women who marry jerks?" I asked my daughter. "Don't forget to talk to your aunt."

"No, that's not my homework," she replied.

"Then what is your homework?"

"Biology, I think."

"Well, how can you figure anything out while watching TV?"

"Dad, can't you see I'm not *watching* TV? I'm trying to do this drawing. Do you happen to know what a leaf looks like?"

"I might be able to help you with that because I once passed through Vermont, but first, I want you to tell me: If you're not watching TV, why is it on?"

"Dad, everyone has the TV on. You don't have to watch it—except your show, of course."

"Neurosurgeons like my show in the background. At least, that's what Nielsen tells me."

Turning off the set, I said, "Okay, let's see if we can remember what a leaf looks like."

Staring at me uneasily, she said, "It's so *quiet*. How can I work when it's so quiet?"

"I wonder why libraries don't have rhumba bands."

"Libraries are different: you can hang out with your friends. The books are around in case nobody shows up."

"Honey, just listen for a moment: what you're hearing now is called silence. There used to be a lot of it in the world until about 1973, when most of it went right out the ozone hole. But if you can find any of the little that's left, it's still the best accompaniment for work. Thomas Jefferson had it when he wrote the Declaration of Independence. If he'd been watching 'Dance Party,' he might have written, *All men are created awful*."

"Can I at least phone someone?"

"You think Lincoln wrote the Gettysburg Address while he was on hold?"

"Dad, those were the olden days, when you were a kid. Things are much better now: Lincoln could *fax* that address to Gettysburg."

Mindlessly, she reached over and flipped on her stereo; and suddenly, she came alive, as if sniffing oxygen.

"Yes! Whitney, let's work!"

"When Whitney Houston makes a record," I said, "is she also listening to a tape of you?"

"Dad, are you trying to make some point?"

"Yes: it's best to do one thing at a time. Can't you see that now?"

She would have seen had she been listening to me, but she was lost in the music. At least I had the comfort of knowing that her homework would be background for it—her homework and perhaps a soccer match.

6

///

They're Taking a Field Trip to France

In Mary Channing Wister, a school full of ancient absolutes and original insults, teachers taught certain disciplines that seem comically quaint today. For example, the average American child today has figured out how to sit down, but at Mary Channing Wister we needed lessons. Although learning how to sit down should have been an elective, it was a grimly required course, one taught in an assembly that belonged at Fort Dix.

First, all of us marched into the auditorium in a column of twos, each of us holding another child's hand; and some of those hands belonged to girls who acted as though they were holding toxic waste.

"Why's your hand always so sweaty?" said Sandra to me one day as we made another forced march.

"How you know that's comin' from me?" I replied. "You're in there too, y' know."

"Only *boys* sweat."

I had a feeling she was wrong, but science hadn't been my best subject.

As soon as all of us had marched into the auditorium and were standing over our seats, the vice-principal said, "All right, children . . . face *front* . . . hands on seats . . . *place* . . . and *silently* lower."

An impressive number of students managed to find their seats and lower them without looking, but others had to turn around.

"I believe I told you all to face front," said the vice-principal. "All right, everybody, let's try it again. Raise all lowered seats . . . At attention now . . . facing me . . . Ready . . . silently . . . still facing front . . . hands on seats . . . place."

On a good day, when all the kids were awake, it took us less than ten minutes to sit down. On a bad day, however, sitting down became the heart of the assembly program.

"I heard too many seats," the vice-principal would say. "You're not in a restroom. We will try it again."

"Stop banging the toilet, Cosby," said a large boy named Bernie one morning. "You'll keep us here all day."

"It's not me, you jerk," I told him.

"*Nobody* calls me a jerk. Meet me in the yard after school."

"I can't fight in my school clothes."

"You'll need good clothes for your funeral."

"Okay, I'll be there," I said, wondering if it would be possible to change into something casual first so that my mother wouldn't be beating up whatever Bernie had missed.

The fight was longer than Harold's with Eddie but shorter than the Louis-Schmelling rematch. At Mary Channing Wister, after-school fighting was a varsity sport and Bernie already had his letter. What I did better was fight back tears as I sprinted home in excellent time, more aware than ever that track was my sport. I would simply have to remember to start my running *before* the next fight.

When I reached my house, my father was there and he welcomed me.

"What the hell happened to you?"

"Bernie beat me up," I said.

"How come you let him do that?"

"It wasn't my idea. He did it on his own."

"Okay, now here's what I want you to do: I want you to go right back and beat him up."

"He sure won't be expecting that."

"Right. You'll catch him by surprise."

"Yeah, he'll be surprised I wanna get killed again."

"Look, I don't want to be ashamed of you; I want you to be a man. If you don't go back there and beat that guy up, I'm gonna beat you up."

"Why don't you just beat *him* up? Then it comes out even."

At this moment, my mother came into the room and looked in horror at my torn pants, the pants with six inches of hem tucked underneath so I'd be able to wear them for the next five or ten years.

"Look at those pants," she said. "Your good ones. I told you to play carefully."

"He wasn't playin', he was fightin'," said my father. " 'Course, the way he fights, it's playin'."

"Well, you're gonna be punished for ruinin' your school clothes like that," said my mother.

And so, I now was facing a remarkable *triple* jeopardy: I had a chance to be killed first by Bernie, and then by my father, and then by my mother, after which my grandmother might want to make a soup with the bones.

Pondering a life that was about to end at the age of eleven, I walked slowly out of the house, but instead of returning to school to find Bernie, I went to Harold's.

"I gotta stay here a day or two," I told him. "Some people want to kill me an' they're my parents. Listen, did your father tell you to go back an' beat up Eddie after your fight?"

"I told my father I won," said Harold. "He was really proud of me."

Reminding Bernie that he was a jerk was not my biggest mistake in that school. My biggest was scoring high on the IQ test and thus placing myself in a special class that only a Trappist monk would have enjoyed.

Had I done badly on that test, I might have been put in the average class, which often walked past the stifling room where I was endlessly bent over work to realize my potential. But how bright could I have been? I revealed this potential to people who were eager to torture me for it.

It was bad enough to be dripping sweat into an algebra book, but it was unbearable to look up from solving for X and see the average IQs passing our room on their way to the zoo, where nothing isosceles existed. These kids, of course, did not always go to the zoo: one day they went to the airport and took a short flight; and one day they went to New Jersey just to look at cows. It seemed that there was something uplifting for a city boy to look at cows, though I'm not sure how much the sight could have done for some of my friends. Harold, for example, needed more uplift than any herd could provide.

"Where are those lucky guys goin' today?" he whispered to me one morning while watching another field trip depart.

"To Europe, I think," I replied.

"William, no talking," said Mrs. McKinney. "I want to tell this class right now that I'm *very* disappointed by the way you behaved with the substitute yesterday. She told Mrs. Creamer that she may leave teaching."

We had, however, allowed that woman to live, a condition not always guaranteed for substitutes. Because of the pressure to learn felt by those of us with high IQs, the arrival of a substitute was a pleasant break, like a furlough from jail, for a substitute often spent half the period making sure that she was in the right building.

"Class, I'm Mrs. Paganelli," the substitute for Mrs. McKinney had said, "and I could use your help."

"We haven't had that yet," said Sandra, perhaps a beat too soon.

"Let's begin by telling me your names."

"We haven't had that yet."

"By the way, does anyone know where the blackboard is?"

"We're supposed to go outside now, Mrs. Pinelli."

"*Paganelli.* Outside? Now?"

"Yeah, we're studying the outside."

"You mean the buildings or the sky?"

"Whatever's out there."

Of all the substitutes who staggered through that school, the most memorable was a woman named Mrs. Delaney, who one day was explaining crop rotation at the same time that a boy beside me, Theodore Parham, was explaining the screwball to me.

"Young man," she suddenly told him, "stop talking."

Theodore considered her advice for a couple of seconds and decided to ignore it, feeling that the rotation of the ball was more important than that of the crops.

"Young man," said Mrs. Delaney, interrupting her lesson again, "didn't I just tell you to stop talking? Now if I see you talking again, I'm going to give you an F."

A hum ran through the class: Theodore was about to flunk spring planting.

Once more, Mrs. Delaney returned to her rotating crops, and once more Theodore returned to rotating his gums.

"You gotta twist your wrist like *this* to make it break the other way," he told me, gripping an orange from his lunch.

"You!" cried Mrs. Delaney. "What's your name?"

Even though Theodore managed to answer this question correctly, Mrs. Delaney said, "Parham, that's an F."

In spite of this grim grade, Theodore still was more concerned with finding the seams of the orange.

"See, it'll break *away* from a lefty," he told me.

"All right, Parham," said Mrs. Delaney, "that's five more Fs!"

Theodore now had six Fs, enough to fail an entire freshman year, enough to make a student forget about a career in medicine or law and consider a career in valet parking. At this point, one would have expected him to begin pleading for mercy, but he continued to talk.

"All right, Parham, that's a *hundred* Fs!"

The woman was giving a new dimension—one Einstein had missed—to the marking system. When she had reached a thousand Fs, I looked at Theodore with awe, as if I were watching someone who was climbing Mount Everest, though climbing was not precisely the word.

When he had been given a thousand Fs, I began to worry that they might have been enough to send him to jail. And then, at last, he stopped talking, but only because he had finished explaining the screwball to me.

For some reason, Theodore was never angry at Mrs. Delaney while his Fs ranneth over. I, on the other hand, once considered killing a teacher named Mr. Grebs.

I had been sitting at my desk in Mr. Grebs's classroom, minding my own business, quietly doing some supplementary reading called *Wonder Woman*.

"Cosby!" he suddenly cried. "Is that a comic book you're reading?"

What a foolish question from an educated man. He certainly must have known that *Wonder Woman* wasn't the story of Eleanor Roosevelt.

"Well . . . yes and no," I replied.

"You can't narrow it down any more than that?" he said, moving toward me. "Tell you what, Cosby: I wouldn't want anything to happen to this precious book of yours, so I'll keep it safe for you for the rest of the year."

And he snatched it from my hands, just moments before I would learn if Wonder Woman was going to save the entire earth, or at least Philadelphia. I was now very angry, for Mr. Grebs had embarrassed me in front of my friends.

When I came home from school that day, my mother responded to my mood.

"Why you so mad?" she said.

"Mr. Grebs took away my book," I replied.

"Why'd he do that?"

"Beats me."

"We may get to that. What book?"

"*Wonder Woman*," I said softly, as if in prayer.

"What'd you say? *Wonders of the World?*"

"No, *Wonder Woman*."

"*Wonder Woman?* Why'd you take that to school? I swear, *I'm* Wonder Woman for putting up with you."

It seemed that my mother was on Mr. Grebs's side. As a member of another generation, one that read books whose dialogue was not in balloons, my mother felt that *Wonder Woman* was worthless. She was, of course, wrong: it was worth a lot to me then, and today, a 1946 comic book could be listed on the American Exchange.

In the following days, I was desperate to take revenge against Mr. Grebs. I was considering sneaking into his room before class and writing on the blackboard GREBS IS A BASTERD; but I wasn't sure if that was the spelling or if the spelling was *bastid,* and I didn't want to get a bad mark in English.

Inspiration, however, suddenly struck: I would walk closely behind Mr. Grebs in the hallway and then step on the back of one of his heels so that his whole shoe came off. To me, this was the funniest joke that you could play on anyone (my sense of humor still needed work) and I played it well: I had often removed a shoe from a boy as neatly as if I had been a salesman at Thom McAn.

And so, one morning in the hallway, I placed myself at the heels of the biggest heel I knew, trying to muster the courage to take one small step for mankind. For several tense seconds, I trailed him—and then my place-kicking foot made its move. The next thing I knew, I was on top of him and he was on the floor, still wearing both shoes, while some of the kids were laughing.

"He didn't have the ball!" one of them cried.

"Fifteen yards for clipping!" cried another.

"Tell you what, Cosby," said Mr. Grebs with a chilling smile. "Let's see if we can find a comic book that can teach you how to walk."

Less than a year after Mr. Grebs and I had hit the deck together, I learned that I could make people laugh with my mouth as well as my feet. I was sitting in Mrs. McKinney's class when I happened to hear her say, "You know, children, storytelling goes all the way back to caveman times. Is there anyone here who would like to come up and tell us a story?"

"About cavemen?" said Fat Albert.

"No, about something real in your lives that's entertaining."

I flung my hand into the air.

"Yes, William, you have one?" she said with a smile.

"Yeah, about how much he loves his father's pants when his father ain't in 'em," said Harold, and a few people laughed. They were laughing *at* me. Could I make them laugh *with* me instead?

"I got a story about sleepin' with my brother," I said.

"You always sleep with your brother, William?"

"Well, I get in bed with him, but there ain't much sleepin'."

The laughter I heard had changed its direction.

"Fine. You come right up here and see if you can make a good story out of bedtime with your brother. And try to do it without saying *ain't*."

As I walked to the front of the room, I felt a command I never had known in the sixty-yard dash. Now, facing the first audience of my life, I smiled at one of the girls and then said, "I share a bed with my little brother, but he's not little enough."

Mrs. McKinney and a few of the kids laughed and the laughter hit me like a drug. With another smile and a stronger voice, I said, "Y' see, he keeps touchin' me an' I don't like a bed that feels like a bus."

After my second laugh had come, I said, "An' sometimes he does more than just *touch* me. He thinks the bed is a boxing ring, but he never goes to a neutral corner."

Again they laughed. It was even a sweeter sound than the tinkle of change in my father's pants. And it was the only vocational guidance that I would ever need.

Children today seem to need considerably more guidance than I received. In fact, the heart of the modern school is not the cafeteria or the parking lot: it's the detention room, a minimum-security lounge designed to teach ethics to kids while keeping their social contacts fresh.

"Detention was really fun today," my son Ennis once told me, as if talking about a yacht club. "All the best people were there."

"I thought it was supposed to be for *punishment*," I said.

"Oh, it can be for that too—if your friends aren't there or if Mrs. Piano is in a bad mood."

"She's the warden?"

"That's funny, Dad. They'd love you in detention because they love to have a good laugh."

"Yes, every prison needs some laughs. Tell me, why did you happen to get this particular honor today?"

"Dad, detention isn't anything bad."

"Sorry; I've been confused. So why were you invited to cocktails there?"

"Dad, you kill me."

"Don't rule it out."

"Well, *today's* detention—"

"You get it every day?"

"I told you: it's nothing bad. Maybe it was in the Middle Ages, but believe me, it's changed."

"I believe you."

"Today I got it just for throwing a book at James in history. Can you imagine that? Mr. Weinstock gave it to me just for throwing a book. I mean, a *grenade* I could understand."

"Just for throwing your history book."

"Oh no, I don't have one of those."

"You're waiting for it to come as the Book-of-the-Month?"

"No, I lent it to Aaron."

"*And*?"

"Well, he's trying hard to remember what he did with it. We've definitely ruled out his locker 'cause there's no more room in there; and he doesn't think he left it at the mall."

"That's where I'd look for it."

"Anyway, Dad, I gotta tell ya the really great thing that happened there today. Jenny and George both got detention together. And they're going steady, y' see—"

"Like Bonnie and Clyde."

"Shakespeare, right?"

"Whatever."

"Anyhow, Jenny and George, they're two of the regulars, but mostly not together: one of 'em usually takes it free period and the other one after school. But today they were in sync."

"A penal *Madame Butterfly*."

"Shakespeare, right?"

"I'll look it up."

"Well, in the middle of the period, Jenny wrote George a note saying how much she loves him, and Mrs. Piano got her hands on it and she wanted to give him detention, but he already *had* it."

"A problem for the High Court. Does the Constitution protect you against getting detention in detention? Is it double jeopardy?"

"Dad, we're not talking about a quiz show here. Anyhow, George did something beautiful: he took the blame."

"How could he do that?"

"He said *he* wrote the note."

"But it was to him. He said he wrote a love letter to himself? You get more than detention for that."

"Well, it worked. It got Mrs. Piano mixed up, so she didn't add any more detention."

"She probably wanted to be home by dinner."

"That's the kind of stuff that happens in detention, Dad. It's a great place to do schoolwork, if you ever have any, but you can also have some laughs."

"I can't image why a student would want to be anywhere else."

"You're probably kidding, but neither can I."

7

Was Tarzan a Three-Bandage Man?

Jn the days before athletes had learned how to incorporate themselves, they were shining heroes to American kids. In fact, they were such heroes to me and my friends that we even imitated their walks. When Jackie Robinson, a pigeon-toed walker, became famous, we walked pigeon-toed, a painful form of locomotion unless you were Robinson or a pigeon.

"Why you walkin' like that?" said my mother one day.

"This is Jackie *Robinson's* walk," I proudly replied.

"There's somethin' wrong with his shoes?"

"He's the fastest man in baseball."

"He'd be faster if he didn't walk like that. His mother should make him walk right."

A few months later, when football season began, I stopped imitating Robinson and began to walk bow-legged like a player named Buddy Helm.

"Why you always tryin' to change the shape of your legs?" said my mother. "You keep doin' that an' they'll fall off—an' I'm not gettin' you new ones."

Although baseball and football stars inspired us, our real heroes were the famous prize fighters, and the way to emulate a fighter was to walk around with a Band-Aid over one eye. People with acne walked around that way too, but we hoped it was clear that we were worshipping good fists and not bad skin.

The first time my mother saw me being Sugar Ray, not Jackie Robinson, she said, "What's that bandage for?"

"Oh, nuthin'," I replied.

"Now that's a new kinda stupid answer. That bandage gotta be coverin' somethin'—besides your entire brain."

"Well, it's just for show. I wanna look like Sugar Ray Robinson."

"The fastest man in baseball."

"No, that's a different one."

"You doin' Swiss Family Robinson next?"

"Swiss Family Robinson? They live in the projects?"

"You'd know who they are if you read more books instead of makin' yourself look like an accident. Why can't you try to imitate someone like Booker T. Washington?"

"Who does he play for?"

"Bill, let's put it this way: you take off that bandage right now or I'll have your father move you up to stitches."

The following morning on the street, I dejectedly told the boys, "My mother says I gotta stop wearin' a bandage. She wants my whole head to show."

"What's wrong with that woman?" said Fat Albert. "She won't let you do *nuthin*'."

"It's okay, Cos," said Junior, " 'cause one bandage ain't enough anyway. My brother says the really tough guys wear two."

"One over each eye?" I asked him.

"Or one eye and one nose," he said.

"Man, I wouldn't want to mess with no two-bandage man," said Eddie.

And perhaps the toughest guys of all wore tourniquets around their necks. We were capable of such attire, for we were never more ridiculous than when we were trying to be tough and cool. Most ridiculous, of course, was that our hero worshipping was backwards: we should have been emulating the men who had *caused* the need for bandages.

My mother did not understand that pretending to be tough was just another part of creative play for us. Boys today do not deliberately make themselves look like outpatients; and they also are too sensible to play bunkies up, a penalty inflicted on the losers of other games. If you had lost one of those games, you would walk to a wall, lower your pants, lean against the wall, and have the winner throw a ball at you. Far across the Atlantic, British boys who'd lost games were bowing to the winners and saying, "Well played, sir." But in the city that started the Revolution, we were standing with our pants at half-mast and saying, "Not *baseballs,* you bastards!"

In the grand tradition of American sport, the winners celebrated their victories by pelting the losers with anything from snowballs to Spaldeens; but even outlaws like us knew that there was a certain lack of form in throwing a brick at a friend's behind.

One day, after losing a game of handball to Eddie, I found myself up against the wall as his half-dressed target. Eddie, however, pitched bunkies up as if he were helping the Phillies stay in last place. After his fourth throw had missed me, he turned to the bullpen.

"Junior's gonna throw for me," he said.

"Oh no!" I cried. "No relief pitchin'."

"Well, I'm used t' pitchin' to the other side. Your ass is too small."

"Tough; that's the strike zone."

At last, he managed to hit me with a changeup, but my mother happened to see it, and a few minutes later, she was doing color commentary on the event:

"Don't you ever take off your pants on the street again, you *hear*? You ever see your *father* doin' that?"

"Well, he don't play too much bunkies up."

*   *   *

Do kids today ever take a break from throwing
Wiffle balls and Frisbees to throw a boomerang? I still
remember the day when Junior Barnes brought an au-
thentic boomerang down to the street, a thing none of
us had ever seen.

"It's a magic weapon," he said. "You throw it at
somebody an' it comes back to you."

"You mean you try to hit a guy an' you hit yourself?"
said Harold. "That's really dumb."

"Look, they use it in Austria, so go ask the Austri-
anos. I just know they throw it at their enemies an'
then it comes back."

"But all the enemies gotta do is follow it back an'
they know where you are."

"Yeah," said Fat Albert. "It's like they was throwin'
it at you even though you is throwin' it at them."

Tired of exploring aeronautics with airheads, Junior
suddenly cocked his arm, leaned back, and hurled the
boomerang down the street. It was a magnificent throw,
a flight that rose and turned left above a Chinese laundry and disappeared.

"Okay, whadda we do now?" said Eddie.

"Wait for it to come back," Junior replied.

And so we all sat down and waited for the boomerang
to return. After about five minutes, Harold said, "Maybe
you gotta be in Austria for the thing to come back."

Junior, however, insisted that we keep our watch,
but after another five minutes, I said, "Hey, I'll go look

for it. You guys stay here just in case I don't see it passin' me comin' back."

As I dashed down the street, I kept searching the sky, until I stopped at the corner and asked a woman, "Miss, did you happen to see a boomerang? It went by that laundry a few minutes ago an' it hasn't come back."

"Lots o' things don't come back from that laundry," she said.

"Listen, miss, d' ya happen to know how far a boomerang gotta go before it turns around an' comes back?"

When she said that it probably was lost, I returned to the boys and found them wrestling with a new scientific challenge: how to lift a nickel up through an iron sidewalk grate by using a chewed piece of Topps on a string. The creativity of my boyhood was endless, but perhaps an end should have come before we turned to bubble gum banking.

Presiding over this low finance was Junior, who was telling his fellow fishermen as I rejoined the group, "Look, we gotta use a magnet."

"I once tried a magnet," said Eddie, "an' it don't work on nickels."

"You musta used the wrong kinda magnet—or the wrong kinda nickel."

"The nickel's gotta be heads *up*," said Fat Albert, who had never assumed that position himself.

Turning to Harold, who was straining to attach the bait to the coin, Eddie said, "And that's the wrong kinda gum; it's too hard. Ya gotta chew it a lot an' then get it down there real fast while it's sticky."

"Well, I don' gotta bring it up for that," said Harold. "I'll just soften it up down there."

And Weird Harold, the most perfectly named man since Ivan the Terrible, began to spit through the grate.

"I'll help ya," said Junior, for whom spitting was an Olympic event.

"Me too," said Fat Albert, the president of a saliva bank.

"If that nickel ever comes up," I said, "I don't wanna touch it unless I get a shot."

Having forgotten about what Junior had launched in the upper air, the four of them were now happily polluting the air below. Their grasp of physics was still slippery, but their talent for turning something dumb into fun was as strong as it had ever been. If a child today went fishing for a coin through a grate, he would probably be using Krazy Glue instead of having a crazy time.

The sharpest contrast between my childhood and the childhood of today can be seen at Halloween, the most sacred holiday for Junior, Eddie, Harold, Fat Albert, and me. Each Halloween of my adulthood, children come to my house in costumes made in a scary place called Taiwan. They are little collection agencies flaunting their packaged cuteness at me.

"Trick or treat!" they cry, hoping for candy, coins, or antiques.

"I'll take the trick," I reply, knowing my home is insured.

There is now a moment of silence while the angels of extortion try to understand the change in the script.

"No," says one of them, as if I'm hard of hearing, "trick or *treat*."

"Right; I'll take the trick. Let me have it. I was in the armed forces."

"But . . . we don't have one."

"Let me get this straight. You're giving me a meaningless choice because your threat is purely hypothetical?"

"C'mon, give us the candy."

"Don't you want to throw anything at me besides an empty threat?"

"Well, what can you give us to throw?"

"Nobody has a stocking with flour?"

"We didn't bring any flowers."

"Look, at least stick a pin in my doorbell."

"What does that do?" says one of them.

"You got a pin?" says another.

But oh, what grand goblins the five of us were in the days before Halloween was just a predictable shakedown. And when Halloween of 1949 arrived, we were yearning to go beyond mere pedestrian property damage to something more admirable. A smashed window here, a small fire there, a woman whose coronary rhythm was turned to ragtime—all these achievements had been fine when we were younger, but when we hit our teens, we heard a higher calling.

And then we saw it, parked near the corner of our

street: a blue Crosley, one of the lightest little cars ever made. Since it was also one of the ugliest, it cried out to be part of Halloween.

"Hey, let's lift that car!" said Junior.

"Steal it?" said Fat Albert.

"No, lift it *up* an' put it someplace else."

"I think that car belongs to somebody," said Harold with his sharp insight into human affairs.

"Yeah, that could be," said Junior. "But we ain't really stealin' it: we're just parkin' it in a better place."

"We're gonna look kinda suspicious carryin' a car," I told him.

"That's why we gotta do it carefully," he said.

And so the five of us picked up that Crosley and began walking down the street with it.

"Wait a minute," said Junior after we had gone about ten feet. "Stop the car. We gotta put it down."

Had an intelligent thought finally slipped into Junior's mind? No, it had not.

"Somebody might see us doin' this," he said.

"That's what I *toldja*," I said. "You start carryin' a car somewhere an somebody's gonna look at you."

"Cos, go in an' get a bedspread."

"But my mother'll—"

"C'mon, we gotta cover this car so nobody sees what it is."

Torn by a desire to please Junior and a desire to avoid death from my mother, I ran into my house and was delighted to find her gone. I wondered which bedspread she would not miss. She slept in her own bed every night and probably remembered the way it looked, but my room was so messy that I might be able to get away with removing my bedspread for a while. I would simply have to figure out how to explain the axle grease to her.

A few minutes later, the car was covered. A bedspread definitely improved the look of a Crosley.

"Where we goin' with it?" said Eddie as we continued to carry the car down the street.

"We better get a story for the police," said Harold, "in case they ask us why we're doin' this."

"It ain't really stealin' a car if nobody got a license to drive it," said Fat Albert, our Philadelphia lawyer.

"We ain't stealin' it," said Junior. "Just puttin' it on the other corner."

"And why we doin' that?" said Eddie.

"I'll think of a reason," Junior told him.

When we had reached the other corner, we were about to put the car down when Junior suddenly pointed to a mailbox and cried, "Let's put it on this!"

At once, we lowered the Crosley and it fit so neatly that it seemed to have been made for display on a mailbox. As if unveiling the new 1950 line, I pulled off the bedspread with a flourish and we all began to laugh.

"I sure hope the owner comes before the mailman picks it up," said Harold.

"Naw, the mailman won't take nuthin' without stamps," said Fat Albert, delivering what had to be the last word.

*   *   *

In those days, when Nintendo was just a town near Rome, my friends and I had recreational *imagination*. For example, one day near the end of December of 1944, we dragged some old Christmas trees to an empty lot, set them on fire, and then threw in cans of beans that exploded and became the world's tastiest grenades. We made these grenades during World War II, when my friends and I were bravely guarding the home front, no matter what the risk might have been; and each of us was well aware that every time we tossed a can of beans into the fire, there was a chance that one of our mothers would get a telegram from the War Department:

WE REGRET TO INFORM YOU THAT YOUR SON, WEIRD
HAROLD, HAS BEEN KILLED IN ACTION BY PORK
AND BEANS ON THE FRONT AT ELEVENTH AND ARCH.

In those ancient days, so many wondrous diversions came not from stores but simply our simple minds. We knew that a trolley was more than just something to carry people around: it could also flatten money. A Toys "Я" Us kid can't imagine what possible use a penny could have, but my friends and I knew that if you put a penny on the tracks and then let a trolley pass over it, you didn't have a penny anymore, you had a copper Rorschach test.

What a vivid picture I still have of the first penny I ever put on the tracks: the fastest devaluation of money since the stock market had crashed. And a few days later, the drama grew even richer: a boy named

Arnold Crane wanted more proof that the trolley was running well, even though he clearly was off his own, so he put a dead mouse on the tracks and performed a public dissection.

"This is really gonna help me become a doctor," he said.

Unfortunately, he became a bookie.

While I was wondering about my own career— How much money could be made in high jumping?— I earned my first income by shining shoes. I made a shoeshine box from an orange crate, borrowed a rag that my mother didn't know she had lent me, and bought some brown polish with the little money I had. If somebody wanted a shine for black shoes, I would simply do the best I could and hope that he didn't look down too much.

At four o'clock one afternoon, outside my building in the projects, I set up my stand with a sign:

SHINE—5 CENTS

Even though all the copy in my advertising was spelled correctly, I had made a major business mistake by failing to study the market. Anyone in the projects who happened to have a nickel was not going to use it to shine his shoes. And so, in my first half hour at work, the only person who stopped at my stand was Junior, who hadn't shined his shoes since 1945.

"How's business?" he said.

"I'll tell ya when I get some," I replied.

"Well, you're shinin' in the wrong place."

"Whaddaya mean? I'm doin' the feet, ain't I?"

"No, the wrong place in the city. You need a place with a lotta guys—like the burlesque house on Arch. A whole lotta guys keep goin' in there an' they're all wearin' shoes."

"What's a burlesque house?"

"Where women take off their clothes."

"Like a locker room?"

"But guys can watch. An' another thing: you're chargin' too much. How ya gonna get tips askin' a whole nickel? You gotta make the people feel *sorry* for ya."

"Maybe I should have a crutch or somethin'."

"Yeah, maybe. Y' see, nobody in the projects feels sorry for ya 'cause they're all in worse shape."

About an hour later, I relocated my non-profit operation to the sidewalk outside the burlesque house at Tenth Street and Arch, and I cut my price to three cents, a dramatic bargain, for the supper-show price should have been higher. The price, however, turned out to be irrelevant because all my potential customers were so eager to go inside that none of them wanted to stop for a shine. They just didn't care how their feet looked to the ladies in the locker room.

Only one man stopped, and he didn't want a shine.

"Just brush 'em off," he said.

"Okay," I told him, "that's two cents."

When I had finished, he gave me two pennies and then began walking away.

"Hey, mister," I said. "No *tip*?"

"Sure," he called back to me. "Drink your milk."

*　　*　　*

The following day, a Saturday, my mother said to me at breakfast, "How's your shoeshine business comin' along?"

"Well, that's what I gotta tell ya," I said. "Y' see, I don't just do anybody's shoes; I pick 'em carefully. So it could be a few years before I can pay for the pants I ripped."

"I see," she said gravely.

Handing her the pennies that represented my business' total cash flow, I said, "But here's two cents for starters."

And then she gave me the smile that might have been my favorite sight.

"Well, it's a very good thing that at least you been tryin'. An' speakin' of tryin', I got a nice surprise for you: let's try on a new suit I got for you last night—one you won't be usin' for football, right?"

"Mom, I'd *love* to try on a new suit, but right now it just so happens I gotta play basketball."

"Down at the park?"

"No, down at the corner."

"At the corner? They build a basketball court there when I wasn't lookin'?"

"We use a trash can."

"I don't want you playin' in garbage."

"Just for layups. An' most of 'em, we bank off the building."

"Well, just try this on for me real quick before you go," she said, grabbing a nearby box and opening it.

"A Robert Hall beauty for Easter."

"Okay, but quick," I said, slipping into a light blue suit jacket, but not all the way. "Hey, ain't my hands supposed to show?"

"You'll grow into it—an' don't say *ain't.*"

"Then why don't I wait an' wear it when I grow into it?"

"It's perfect right now," said the woman who could have tailored the emperor's new clothes.

All of the other mothers, however, had the same remarkable vision, for their sons were a sartorial search for tomorrow, with their necks moving freely in billowing collars and their sleeves revealing just the proper amount of knuckle.

"Okay!" I said, tearing off the jacket and turning toward the front door.

"Just lemme see how the pants—"

"Later!" I cried, dashing out of the house.

With my eye already on the trash can in which I'd be scoring at least thirty points, I did not happen to see my bicycle blocking the front door. When I hit it, the bike and I went down together in a bang that rang through the halls of the building.

"Quiet down there!" came a cry. "I'm tryin' to get some sleep!"

"Well, I'm lyin' down *myself,*" I replied.

"Bill, you okay?" said my mother, running to me.

"Oh, sure," I said, rising slowly. "I know how to fall. All the champions do."

"They learn it by runnin' into their bikes?"

8

//

Go Deep to the Sewer

The essence of childhood, of course, is play, which my friends and I did endlessly on streets that we reluctantly shared with traffic. As a daring receiver in touch football, I spent many happy years running up and down those asphalt fields, hoping that a football would hit me before a Chevrolet did.

My mother was often a nervous fan who watched me from her window.

"Bill, don't get run over!" she would cry in a moving concern for me.

"Do you see me getting run over?" I would cleverly reply.

And if I ever *had* been run over, my mother had a seat for it that a scalper would have prized.

Because the narrow fields of those football games allowed almost no lateral movement, an end run was possible only if a car pulled out and blocked for you. And so I worked on my pass-catching, for I knew I had little chance of ever living my dream: taking a handoff and sweeping to glory along the curb, dancing over the dog dung like Red Grange.

The quarterback held this position not because he was the best passer but because he knew how to drop to one knee in the huddle and diagram plays with trash.

"Okay, Shorty," Junior Barnes would say, "this is you: the orange peel."

"I don' wanna be the orange peel," Shorty replied. "The orange peel is Albert. I'm the gum."

"But let's make 'em *think* he's the orange peel," I said, "an' let 'em think Albert's the manhole."

"Okay, Shorty," said Junior, "you go out ten steps an' then cut left behind the black Oldsmobile."

"I'll sorta go *in* it first to shake my man," said Shorty, "an' then, when he don' know where I am, you can hit me at the fender."

"Cool. An' Arnie, you go down to the corner of Locust an' fake takin' the bus. An' Cos, you do a zig out to the bakery. See if you can shake your man before you hit the rolls."

"Suppose I start a fly pattern to the bakery an' then do a zig out to the trash can," I said.

"No, they'll be expecting that."

I spent most of my boyhood trying to catch passes with the easy grace of my heroes at Temple; but easy grace was too hard for me. Because I was short and thin, my hands were too small to catch a football with arms extended on the run. Instead, I had to stagger backwards and smother the ball in my chest. How I yearned to grab the ball in my hands while striding smoothly ahead, rather than receiving it like someone who was catching a load of wet wash. Often, after a pass had bounced off my hands, I returned to the quarterback and glumly said, "Jeeze, Junior, I don' know what happened." He, of course, knew what had happened: he had thrown the ball to someone who should have been catching it with a butterfly net.

Each of these street games began with a quick review of the rules: two-hand touch, either three or four downs, always goal-to-go, forward passing from anywhere, and no touchdowns called back because of traffic in motion. If a receiver caught a ball near an oncoming car while the defender was running for his life, the receiver had guts, and possibly a long excuse from school.

I will never forget one particular play from those days when I was trying so hard to prove my manhood between the manholes. In the huddle, as Junior, our permanent quarterback, dropped to one knee to arrange the garbage offensively, I said, "Hey, Junior, make me a decoy on this one."

Pretending to catch the ball was what I did best.

"What's a decoy?" he said.

"Well, it's—"

"I ain't got time to learn. Okay, Eddie, you're the

Dr Pepper cap an' you go deep toward New Jersey."

"An' I'll fool around short," I said.

"No, Cos, you fake goin' deep an' then buttonhook at the DeSoto. An' Harold, you do a zig out between 'em. *Somebody* get free."

Moments later, the ball was snapped to him and I started sprinting down the field with my defender, Jody, who was matching me stride for stride. Wondering if I would be able to get free for a pass sometime within the next hour, I stopped at the corner and began sprinting back to Junior, whose arm had been cocked for about fifteen seconds, as if he'd been posing for a trophy. Since Eddie and Harold also were covered, and since running from scrimmage was impossible on that narrow field, I felt that this might be touch football's first eternal play: Junior still standing there long after Eddie, Harold, and I had dropped to the ground, his arm still cocked as he tried to find some way to pass to himself.

But unlimited time was what we had and it was almost enough for us. Often we played in the street until the light began to fade and the ball became a blur in the dusk. If there is one memory of my childhood that will never disappear, it is a bunch of boys straining to find a flying football in the growing darkness of a summer night.

There were, of course, a couple of streetlamps on our field, but they were useful only if your pattern took you right up to one of them to make your catch. The rest of the field was lost in the night; and what an adventure it was to refuse to surrender to that night, to hear the quarterback cry "Ball!" and then stagger around in a kind of gridiron blindman's buff.

"Hey, you guys, dontcha think we should call the game?" said Harold one summer evening.

"Why do a stupid thing like that?" Junior replied.

" 'Cause I can't see the ball."

"Harold, that don't make you special. Nobody can see the ball. But y' *know* it's up there."

And we continued to stagger around as night fell on Philadelphia and we kept looking for a football that could have been seen only on radar screens.

One day last year in a gym, I heard a boy say to his father, "Dad, what's a Spal*deen*?"

This shocking question left me depressed, for it is one thing not to know the location of the White House or the country that gave its name to Swiss cheese, but when a boy doesn't know what a Spal*deen* is, our educational system has failed. For those of you ignorant of basic American history, a Spal*deen* was a pink rubber ball with more bounce than can be imagined today. Baseball fans talk about the lively ball, but a lively baseball is a sinking stone compared to a Spal*deen*, which could be dropped from your eye level and bounce back there again, if you wanted to do something boring with it. And when you connected with a Spal*deen* in stickball, you put a pink rocket in orbit, perhaps even over the house at the corner and into another neighborhood, where it might gently bop somebody's mother sitting on a stoop.

I love to remember all the street games that we could play with a Spal*deen*. First, of course, was stickball, an organized version of which is also popular and known as baseball. The playing field was the same rectangle that we used for football: it was the first rectangular diamond. And for this game, we had outfield walls in which people happened to live and we had bases that lacked a certain uniformity: home and second were manhole covers, and first and third were the fenders of parked cars.

One summer morning, this offbeat infield caused a memorable interpretation of the official stickball rules. Junior hit a two-sewer shot and was running toward what should have been third when third suddenly drove away in first. While the bewildered Junior tried to arrive safely in what had become a twilight zone, Eddie took my throw from center field and tagged him out.

"I'm not out!" cried Junior in outrage. "I'm right here on third!"

And he did have a point, but so did Eddie, who replied, not without a certain logic of his own, "But third ain't *there* anymore."

In those games, our first base was as mobile as our third; and it was a floating first that set off another lively division of opinion on the day that Fat Albert hit a drive over the spot from which first base had just driven away, leaving us without a good part of the right field foul line. The hit would have been at least a double for anyone with movable legs, but Albert's destination was first, where the play might have been close had the right fielder hit the cutoff man instead of a postman.

"Foul ball!" cried Junior, taking a guess that happened to be in his favor.

"You're out of your mind, Junior!" cried Albert, an observation that often was true, no matter what Junior was doing. "It went right over the fender!"

"What fender?"

"If that car comes back, you'll *see* it's got a fender," said Albert, our automotive authority.

However, no matter how many pieces of our field drove away, nothing could ever take away the sweetness of having your stick connect with a Spal*deen* in a magnificent *whoppp* and drive it so high and far that it bounced off a window with a view of New Jersey and then caromed back to the street, where Eddie would have fielded it like Carl Furillo had he not backed into a coal shute.

The balls that kids play with today are simply round, rubberless things that bounce a little, cost a lot, and start to tear after ten days. The Spal*deen*, however, was a ball that belonged in the Arabian Nights, for every pitcher who threw it was a kind of genie.

"Man, did that thing *drop*," said Harold one Saturday morning, admiring Junior's strikeout pitch to Eddie.

"Harold, somebody musta dropped you," said Eddie, walking away from the plate in disgust. "Anybody can make a Spaldeen drop; that's what it *does*."

He had a point: the Spaldeen was the only ball in the history of Philadelphia, or anywhere else, that needed no contribution from the pitcher. In fact, even if a *girl* threw one (and many girls seemed to throw as if they were swatting flies), a Spaldeen still would have done magical things on its way to the plate: it became a split-fingered knuckler. The hardest thing to do in any sport is hit a baseball, but when compared to hitting a Spaldeen, hitting a baseball is like beating a rug.

When a broomstick connected with a Spaldeen, the ball, of course, was not always launched to distant walls. Sometimes it was merely a popup with so much spin that it became an elliptical "egg ball," a wickedly whirling short fly that always popped out of the hands of any fielder who was not a chimpanzee.

The Spaldeen also changed shape when the slam of the stick broke it into halves, an at bat that caused a cry of "Hindoo!" for a moment that had to be replayed. If a base drove away, it was a hindoo; if a bookie grabbed a bouncing hit or an overthrow, it was a hindoo; and if a holy man crossed the field during a play, it was a hindoo, even if he was a Moslem. The Iowa farm boys who grew up playing baseball in their fields of dreams were deprived of the sporting challenges of the city streets, where from time to time steam came out of second base, a hindoo only if there had been a force play in the fog.

The electronic children of today, sitting for hours at their terminals, could not even imagine some of the games that we invented before American children turned into software. If you had ever found *us* at a terminal, we were there to watch girls getting off buses.

Today's kids, for example, could not imagine hoseball, which sounds like a game for demented firemen. In this one, the ball was a five-inch piece of hose that resembled a rubber boomerang. Something inside us (stupidity, I suspect) kept inspiring us to find new balls that behaved as erratically as we did; and hoseball seemed to have been invented by the Three Stooges: not only was the ball erratic but it was angry at you too. Babe Ruth had always been afraid that he would kill a pitcher with a line drive, but in hoseball everyone was Babe Ruth: a ball that bounced off a pitcher's head could carry away a piece of it. Young men in Germany had dueling scars; young men in Germantown had hoseball scabs.

My son grew up swinging at softballs, Wiffle balls, and his sisters. How lost they would have been in the time of boys like me, a boy whose anthem should have been:

Take me out to the ball game;
Take me out to the street.
Pitch me a halfball or rock at my knees;
I'll even swing at a roll with cream cheese.

Yes, we city boys of the late forties had a goofy flair for recycling our environment into recreation. For example, we never put trash in the schoolyard trash can because we used that can for low-level basketball, the game that had upset my mother, a game in which a Munchkin would have been Kareem. Playing above instead of below the basket did tend to produce higher scores. There was, however, no thrill in sport like the one of putting a move on your man, driving to the hoop, and slam dunking into oatmeal.

During all the years that I was a boy, my friends and I said many three-word sentences, such as the simple eloquence of "So's *your* mother!" and "Up yours *too*"; but the three words that none of us ever said were, "Mom, I'm bored." Junior, Harold, Fat Albert, and I could have been moved to the Galápagos Islands and we still would have found endless entertainment. Harold would have started playing marbles with turtle eggs; Junior would have both organized and rigged some turtle races; and I would have studied Fat Albert to see if he was part of the evolutionary chain. But no one ever would have said those three silly words, "Mom, I'm bored" or those foolish five, "Mom, my batteries are dead," for we were charged from within.

A nice illustration was the slightly deranged creativity of a game called buck-buck, which was known in other cities as Johnny-on-the-pony. Five boys lined up, one behind the other, each with his head down and his arms around the waist of the boy in front of him. And as another boy came running toward them, one of them would cry "Buck-buck number one, come in!" and the boy would leap on the horse, where his saddle was somebody's kidney. Then another boy would leap on the horse and another after him, until the horse collapsed. The object of the game was to see how many boys your horse could hold before you went down like a brave bull, a competition that not only was an excellent test of teamwork, but also an excellent way to reshape your spine.

My four closest friends and I had a buck-buck team that belonged in the Calgary rodeo. We were such a sturdy landing pad that we were able to beat teams of boys so tough that their legs had been shortened by constant play, boys with their hats on sideways and toothpicks in their mouths and other wood in their heads.

One day, the leader of one of these fearsome teams tongued his toothpick menacingly at me and said, "We hear you clowns callin' yourselves big buck-buck men."

"There's no bigger," I replied.

"Okay, we challenge you to the buck-buck championship of the world."

"We accept. Not just the world but Philadelphia *too*!"

And so, the five of us lined up, I cried, "Buck-buck number one, come in!" and the challengers began to attack.

The first boy who landed felt to us like part of a building collapse, and Junior then made a suggestion for improving the quality of play:

"Check that bastard's pockets!" he said.

At the risk of breaking the flow of the game, we checked the boy's pockets and found two big rocks.

"What the hell are *these*?" I said, though I was pretty sure I knew.

"They's for balance," he said.

"Well, you want rocks, just keep the ones in your head."

After this lad's rapid weight loss, the game began again. However, even without being stoned, those guys were so big that we were able to hold only three of them before the fourth one took us down.

The pressure was on us now. We had to win with our number-three leaper against five boys who had the bodies of mules.

Our first attacker was Harold, but his landing made no impression.

"What was that?" said part of the horse. "A piece of paper? Somebody throw a piece of paper on me?"

And the rest of the horse started laughing while another one said, "Okay, number two, let's see if you weigh zero too."

Angrily, I took off and landed.

"Another piece of paper!" cried the hind boy. "We must be in a parade."

While our opponents were enjoying their joke, I was enjoying the thought that they were about to lose not only the game but possibly consciousness as well. Our third man was Fat Albert.

Fat Albert had not received his name because of the state of his mind, although lard undoubtedly composed most of his brain. He had received the name as an unnecessary label for his size, which was roughly that of an elephant at birth. And so, when Fat Albert approached the enemy horse—at a moderate speed, of course—Richter scales picked him up; and even though they had no seismographs, those five cocky horsemen could feel him coming and had sudden visions of being the first boys in North Philadelphia to ever die in a stampede.

"We give! We *give!*" cried the rear of the horse after spinning his head around in fear. "Jesus Christ, don't let that thing fall on us!"

I had never known a buck-buck team to end a game in prayer.

Most kids today don't use the street as an amusement park the way my friends and I did. When I was a boy, Super Mario was the guy who fixed our sink; but Super Mario now is a kind of electronic Olympics for kids like the ones next door to me, who sit endlessly staring at a television screen full of blips, as if they were little air-traffic controllers.

While watching three of them recently, I saw a display of hand-eye coordination that made me grateful I was a child when hand-eye coordination was needed only to stick your hand in someone else's eye.

"Stay in the pipe!" cried Brian, age nine, to his sister Molly, age seven, as she handled the Super Mario Bros. 3 control. "Crack the block! Get out of the tornado!"

"How can a tornado get into the pipe?" I asked

their sister Katie, age thirteen.

Looking at me as if the block with the crack was my brain, she replied, "With firepower you can use a mushroom to stay in the air because she's Tanooki Mario, *not* the frog."

"I see," I said with no idea what she was talking about. "Tell me, does this game have an object?"

"Of *course*," said Brian. "You have to rescue the princess."

"From the Communists?"

"No, from the monsters, ghosts, and mini-bosses."

"Mini-bosses? You mean tiny union leaders?"

"Just watch us, it's simple: you have to get through six lands for each world and eight worlds in all. Every time you finish a world, you get a warp whistle."

And so I watched these three children coping with quicksand, demons, blocked pipes, and possibly clogged sinuses too. The only thing I knew for certain was that there was a princess trapped in either a sewer or a zoo.

"Use a Koopa to clear the block!" cried Katie.

"Hey, you know what can *also* clear the block?" I said, trying to join the fun. "A few cherry bombs."

"They can't get you into the next world," said Molly.

"They can if you're close enough."

"Fly with a tail!" she called to Katie, who had taken the control.

"It's okay," said Katie. "He's in a raccoon suit."

"That's better than polyester?" I said.

"Yes, a raccoon suit lets you fly for a whole stage."

"Katie, the shells!" cried Brian. "They're going to kill you. Let *me* do it."

And he grabbed the control from her. She responded by shoving him and he hit her in the back, a rabbit punch that I found warmly nostalgic. No matter how high tech their games, kids were still kids and always would be. In fact, the first kids on the moon will probably broadcast to Earth:

"This is one small step for children, one big step for childhood . . . *Hey,* why'd you *punch* me?"

"Because *I* wanted to say that."

9

///

Take Wing, My Glands

Childhood is full of firsts. The first time you tie your own shoes. The first tooth you leave for the fairy. The first time you gag on broccoli.

And your first love.

Who can ever forget his first love? I could until a few days ago, when I heard Sinatra sing "Nancy With the Laughing Face" and suddenly remembered how painfully I gave my heart to a wee stunner named Nancy Livingston one winter morning when I was ten.

Carrying a pair of hockey skates that my father had gotten for me at a pawnshop, I went out that morning to a nearby pond. I was wearing just a light jacket and a scarf because I wanted to look cool, the way that real ice skaters looked. When I reached the pond, however,

I quickly succeeded in being even more than cool: I was frozen.

My refrigeration had been helped, of course, by falling about twenty-eight times on hands that sometimes missed footballs but consistently caught the ice. When I finally quit skating and sat down to remove what should have been double or triple runners, these hands were as numb as the mind that had brought me to this sport in these clothes. I wanted to do the sensible thing and cry, but all I could manage was a whimper.

"William, are you okay?" said a sweet voice, and I turned and saw Nancy Livingston, the fourth grade's most fabulous face and a featured player in my dreams.

"Oh, sure," I unconvincingly said. "Why *wouldn't* I be?"

" 'Cause you're crying."

"It's just allergies."

"Allergies? In January?"

"It's . . . winter wheat. That's the worst stuff of all. Sometimes the farmers don't stop crying till spring."

"You want to skate with me? I can do a figure eight."

"Hey, I'd love to," said the boy who couldn't do a decimal point, "but I just finished giving a lesson and I gotta take a short break, especially with all this hay fever."

"Okay, see ya," said my secret love, and off she went to skate with somebody who hadn't lost touch with his hands and feet, and also his mind.

Behind Nancy Livingston, I had a backup fantasy.

If I couldn't win Nancy (and I couldn't), I dreamed of winning Wonder Woman, that inspirational comic book heroine who showed me that the American flag could also be a brassiere.

For today's child, bewitched by MTV, comic books have little power, but when I was a boy and there was no lingerie channel, I was in love with Wonder Woman. As I read those stirring pages and looked at her Yankee Doodle thighs, I imagined us married and jumping off buildings together to bring Truth, Justice, and the American Way to North Philadelphia.

"What you doin' under there?" said my father one night as he entered my room, relieved to see that the bed was glowing instead of falling apart.

"Oh, just a little reading," I said, emerging from the blankets with my flashlight. "It helps me relax."

"From *what*? All you ever do is relax." And then his eyes fell on Wonder Woman and they almost fell from his head. "Hey, I've never seen this one."

"Wonder Woman. She goes after the crooks Superman misses."

"Is she somebody else when she's not Wonder Woman? I mean, a hairdresser or somethin'?"

I had never seen my father so interested in fighting crime—except, of course, when he went after me.

"Yeah, she's somethin' else. A woman who can't fly."

"Well, it's time for you to go to sleep now. I'll just take this an' hold it for you till tomorrow."

And off my father went with Wonder Woman, leaving me to dream about one day getting my little hands on her, though something in me knew that those hands would have to keep settling for Wonder Bread.

Children today know more about sex than I *or* my father did. At ten, my daughters probably knew the ideal temperature for conception, but at twelve, I still believed Fat Albert's story that women used Kotex to hold in the babies.

One day last year, I read about a new product called Rubber Ducky Condoms, the first erotic toy specifically made for kids, and I realized how far puberty had come since the days when I misunderstood it. I doubt that kids of twelve today would be sitting on a stoop and listening to the mangled biology of Fat Albert.

And just last week, I was shaken by another newspaper story:

4TH GRADE LAMENT: "EVERYONE'S DATING"

Betsy Davis's son came home from school one day and told her he wanted to take his girlfriend on a date to the movies.

"Girlfriend?" replied Ms. Davis. "You're ten years old."

Looking back now, I can see how lucky I was to have grown up in a time before childhood was repealed, before ten-year-olds were involved in minor-league lust. Childhood romance used to be so tender and innocent in the days before dolls were anatomically correct. In those days, even the *kids* weren't anatomically correct: Junior Barnes once told me it was possible for a man to be trapped in a woman and not be able to get out.

"No kiddin'," I said, frightened by the thought of becoming a permanent part of my first love. "Junior, you know anybody who ever got trapped in there?"

"Guys don't talk about it 'cause they're ashamed of havin' to be rescued," he said, "but it happens all the time—an' not just in the circus."

"You ever . . . *done* it?"

"I guess so."

"Whaddaya mean, you 'guess so'?"

"I'm pretty sure I done it, but I can't remember exactly. That happens sometimes when you're handlin' lots of women."

"I think I done it too," said Fat Albert.

"What're you doing?" said my mother one day when she saw me lifting my weights, which were a couple of bookends.

"Gettin' in shape for girls," I replied.

"You gonna wrestle 'em?"

"No, just look better so they'll go for me."

"It's what's *inside* that counts. Forget the bookends an' read the books."

"But that won't make me look different."

"You'll look smarter."

"Well, I'll have to see if smarter is somethin' they want."

"If the girls're worth anything, they'll want it."

"I don't know if they're worth anything, but they're the only ones around."

The following day at school, I said to a girl in my class, "Hey, Linda, what things do you like in a boy?"

"Well . . . I like John's eyes," she said. "And James's hair. And . . . George's walk."

"Anything of *mine*?"

"Yes, you have a nice smile."

"Does that mean I'm cute?"

"Cuter than some, not as cute as others."

What a ringing testimonial.

"Which parts of me need the most work?"

"Well, you could stand a little straighter. And you could smile more; you have a really nice smile. Keep brushing your teeth."

Encouraged by Linda's critique, I quickly turned myself into a cool composite of sex appeal: I imitated James's hair, George's walk, Roy's shoulders, and John's eyes; I kept only my smile. How did I manage to imitate John's eyes? I had seen that he narrowed them slightly to look at girls, the way Clark Gable did; and so I developed a sensuous squint that moved one girl to say, "Bill, did you lose your glasses?" But at least she was talking to me.

It wasn't easy for me to become this enticing cross-section of manhood, to be constantly remembering to keep my hair brushed a certain way and my shoulders squared and my pectorals flexed and my eyes slightly closed and my knees slightly bent. I also kept smiling for no reason, as if I were a movie star or a blooming idiot.

The renovated Cosby, however, did make an impact on some girls in school. One morning in the hall I was stopped by a semi-pubescent beauty, who looked at me sweetly and said, "Bill, is anything wrong with you?"

"Of course not," I said with surprise. "Don't you see all the things that're *right*?"

"What do you mean?"

"I mean I got a new haircut and a new walk and new shoulders too."

"Well, that's lovely, but don't you see? I just want you to be *you*."

"No, if I'm just myself, I'll never get anyone."

"But I liked the way you were."

"Well, I'm sorry. I can't remember it."

In spite of this girl's remarks, I was eager to test the newly assembled me in a social situation, which came at a party thrown by my friend Eddie. Early one Saturday night when I was twelve, I entered Eddie's apartment, where a few boys and girls were moving uneasily about, for the girls were shy and the boys had the polish of Quasimodo. Fearing that any second I would have to talk to one of those girls, I kept trying to think of a good opening.

Hi there, I'm Bill Cosby. You come here often?

No, really dumb. No one came here often, not even Eddie, who spent most of his time in the street.

Hi there, I'm Bill Cosby. You live around here?

No, she would reply, *I live in Elmira. I just flew down for the night.*

Unfortunately, *Hi there, I'm Bill Cosby,* my strongest material, also was dumb because I knew almost all of these girls from school, where I worked hard to avoid them.

Hi there, I'm Bill Cosby—as everyone knows. Do you like fire drills?

Still not precisely a trip to the moon on gossamer wings.

And so, I was drinking punch and wishing I was home with my picture of Lena Horne when suddenly Nat King Cole started to sing,

> **They tried to tell us we're too young,**
> **Too young to really be in love . . .**

Moved by Cole's silky sounds, I found myself drifting dreamily across the room until my eye was caught by a girl standing alone at the opposite wall. She was pretty, but she also seemed to be at least five feet five and these boys wanted no woman looking down on them. Less from passion than pity, I approached this lonely vision, looked up, and said, "Hi there, I'm Bill Cosby. Wanna dance a little?"

Dancing a little was my style. My mother had taught me a box step that also worked for the rhumba and waltz, but only if the girl had good reflexes.

Without saying a word, she responded by leading me out to the dance floor, where some of my friends were shoving other girls around. She now knew my name, and maybe one day I would know hers. As we began to dance, I took one more try and soulfully said, "You new around here?"

"Mmmm," she replied.

Was that yes or no? Perhaps she didn't know the answer; I was sorry to have asked her such a tough question. She was, however, in tune with the times, for this was the age of non-verbal communication between twelve-year-olds of the opposite sex. All about me, kids were almost dancing with each other: silently, they were holding each other at arm's length, as if there might be communicable disease.

The essence of this detachment was avoiding eye contact. But what did you do with your eyes? Looking at your feet was not only awkward but might send you dancing into a wall. The only solution was to *look* at a wall, each of you at an opposite one, as if you were dancing a bolero.

No wall, however, was needed for me: this particular girl at the end of my arms, whatever her name, was safe from eye contact because I was facing her throat. And whenever my eyes wandered away from this view, they saw my friends making faces at me, while my partner's alternate view was girls giggling at her. The kids in Eddie's living room that night had discovered a great truth: sex is funny, especially for new arrivals.

And then some day they may recall
We were not too young at all.

But we were too young to stop laughing or to have enough poise to exchange names. When the song had ended, Miss Anonymous and I dropped hands, blinked at each other meaningfully, and then turned and went in opposite directions. At the sidelines, each of us was met by friends eager for steamy details.

"So, how *was* she?" said Junior.

"I couldn't begin to tell ya," I said, and this was true: I couldn't begin to tell him because there was nothing to tell.

"You cop a little feel?"

"I was workin' mostly on her shoulders."

"Nothin' with her ears?"

"They was out o' reach."

"Hey, what's her name?"

"Believe me, I'm gonna find out."

A few minutes later, while drinking more punch and wondering how much longer I had to keep having all this fun, I looked at the dance floor and saw Elaine Williams, who had just come to the party. She was the girl who had so addled my crossing guard's brain one day outside of school that I had lovingly sent her through a red light. And now I felt a deep desire to dance with her and recapture the magic of the moment when I had almost sent her under a bus. Elaine was clearly the girl of my dreams. She was my height and I knew her name.

She was dancing with Weird Harold, the equivalent of dancing alone, and so I was full of confidence when

I went to cut in. Tapping Harold on the shoulder, I smilingly said, "May I?"—and suddenly I was knowing the joy of having Elaine trapped in my box step. Harold had left glumly, forced to follow the code of cutting in, the same code I had to follow when he returned in less than a minute to cut back in on me. The code allowed quick counterattack.

Although I surrendered Elaine angrily, I decided to be a good sport and give Harold thirty seconds with her. And then I cut back in on him, probably making Elaine wish that she were back in traffic. Now that I had captured her again, my plan was not to delight her with my syncopated box step but to avoid another attack by Harold; and so, when I saw him coming again, I began to spin away to keep my shoulders a moving target. The dance was a fox trot, but I was doing a pirouette, trying to keep Harold from pinning my shoulders to the wall, while Nat King Cole spoke for us to the girls:

I love you
For sentimental reasons.

During my boxy effort to both woo and hide Elaine, I noticed that some of the other dancers were much closer together now and were imitating the grind of their older friends. Loins were being turned loose, but I was still trying to lose Harold.

"Why are we going into the *kitchen*?" Elaine suddenly said.

"Why not?" I smoothly replied, moving not toward

the grind but the grinder.

And then I said no more. Only a Fred Astaire could have counted steps and made conversation too.

Now that I have fathered four daughters of my own, I think I know how Nancy and Elaine felt; but I may be wrong, for the NBA will play on Pluto before the first father understands the mind of his teenage daughter.

"Mom," said Erinn, my fourteen-year-old, one day to my wife and me, ignoring me, "Debbie just called and I can't believe it: her boyfriend's best friend is coming to a party and she wants me to actually meet him! What do I do with my *hair*?"

"Your hair looks lovely," I said.

"Oh, Daddy, don't you know *anything*?"

Yes, of course I did: I knew the capital of Kentucky and the Vice President's name and the winner of the last Super Bowl, but I decided not to flaunt all this knowledge at a girl who was having a breakdown over an unknown boy.

"When is the party?" said my wife.

"In only three weeks!"

"Look, honey," I said, entering the minefield again, "you shouldn't get so uptight about someone you haven't even seen. He might look like the Swamp Thing and then your hair won't really matter. You'll just have to make sure you have a towel."

"Dad, Debbie and I have known each other for years. She has wonderful taste and she says he's great-looking."

"Then why hasn't he found someone already?"

"He's found *me*."

"Maybe he has, but *I'm* getting lost."

"Let me talk to Mom."

"She's right here; I'll see if she's free. But first, just tell me about his *personality*. Does he have one?"

"I'll know that when I meet him. Mom, what should I wear to draw attention away from my hair?"

It turned out, however, that she should have worn designer knee pads so she could have dropped down from time to time to the boy's height. The day after the party, Erinn said to us in despair, "I'll never be able to show my face in public again. There was so *little* of him."

"You'll find bigger ones," said my wife.

"Honey, you can't judge a man by his height," I told her, showing again the learning disability that all fathers have.

"You can judge how tall he is," she said.

"Well, anyway, I *know* your hair looked lovely—even if he couldn't see it."

10

Or Maybe It's a Spanish Flea

That party at Eddie's now seems to have been my last moment of innocence, a quality that children used to have, before they began going directly from Pablum to the Pill. By the following year, I not only knew how to dance and talk all at once, but my friends and I were in hot pursuit of Spanish Fly, which wasn't something that buzzed in Barcelona.

By the time that I was thirteen, I understood sex, but I was still too short and thin to expect that any girl, no matter how much she liked my smile, would ever surrender to me anything more than her rotating shoulder blades. And then one morning, Junior Barnes told us about Spanish Fly, an aphrodisiac so potent that it could have made Lena Horne surrender to Fat Albert.

"You feed this stuff to a girl and she just goes crazy for you," he said.

"Does she gotta be Spanish?" said Eddie.

"I don't think so," said Junior. "She just gotta be a girl."

"How do you feed it to her?" I asked him. "In a sandwich or somethin'?"

"You gotta slip it to her when she thinks she's drinkin' somethin' else. A coupla drops in her Dr Pepper."

"But you gotta be careful not to give her too much," said Junior, "or she'll go for a flagpole instead o' you."

"Well, how d'ya *know* how much?" I said. "Does it say on the bottle?"

"Soon as her clothes come off, that's enough."

"I heard that even better is ground rhinoceros horn," said Weird Harold.

"Maybe," said Junior, "but it's probably easier to get rhino horn in Africa than Philadelphia. Spanish Fly is the thing, I tell ya."

"So where do we get some?" said Harold.

"Well, my brother knows this guy on Bainbridge who has a deal with the Spanish Navy."

"What's it look like?" I said.

"You can get it *any* way: a powder, a cookie, juice. But it don't matter: either one an' the girl comes flyin' at ya legs first."

"Wow," said Harold in raunchy reverence. "I'd give her a whole *glass*."

"I told ya: too much an' she forgets about you an'

takes on the Navy yard."

While they talked about love, I pictured Dorothy Dandridge sitting on my bed, having beaten Lena Horne there.

Some Spanish Fly, Dorothy? I would graciously say.
Love some, she'd reply.
With or without ice?
Do you happen to have the drops?
Of course. Eye or nose?

"What does it cost?" said Eddie, snapping me back to reality.

"A lot," said Junior. "This stuff ain't Juicy Fruit."

"You think they trade for baseball cards?" said Harold.

"No, I think those Spanish sailors want money. But if we pool all we got . . ."

Early that evening, Junior reconvened the family-life class at the sewer, collected nine dollars and sixty cents from Eddie, Harold, Fat Albert, and me, and then led us off in search of Spanish Fly. We were feeling the way that the soldiers of Ponce de León must have felt when they began to search for the Fountain of Youth. Of course, they probably already had plenty of Spanish Fly, in case they ran into any sleeping señoritas on the way.

"I got a new plan," said Junior as we walked to the trolley to take us downtown. "My brother hasn't seen the guy on Bainbridge lately, so he says we should go right to the Navy yard an' look for Spanish sailors."

A challenge indeed now lay ahead, for most of the Spanish sailors in America were hanging around in 1610, but we had the resourcefulness of city kids of the forties.

When we reached the big Navy yard, we found a sentry booth with a sailor who was probably guarding a secret supply of Spanish Fly. Nervously, we planned our attack.

"Junior, you talk to him," said Harold. "You're good at askin' for Spanish Fly."

"But he's an *American* sailor," said Eddie. "He wouldn't know."

"Maybe we better go back," said Fat Albert, "an' just wait till the girls're in the mood."

"They're never in the mood for us," I said. "They need chemicals."

"Okay," said Junior, "I'll make the deal. You guys cover me."

"If my father ever catches me here . . ." said Harold.

"Don't worry, man," I told him. "It's your *mother* who looks for sailors," an observation I would not have made when I was twelve and knew nothing about women.

Bravely approaching the sailor, Junior now said, "Don't shoot, I'm American!"

"Hey, so am I," the sailor replied. "What's your business, American?"

"My friends an' I . . . well, see, we got a school science project and . . . well, to get really good marks, we could use some . . ." He smiled knowingly at the sailor, who smiled in bewilderment at him. "Some . . ." And he dropped his voice to a whisper so that no spies would overhear. "Spanish Fly."

"Danish rye?"

"No, Spanish Fly."

The sailor laughed. "How much do you need?"

"Enough for our grade—for the *project,* that is. We can pay for it."

"Yeah? How much?"

"Nine dollars and sixty cents."

"Well, I just happen to have nine dollars and sixty cents' worth right here. I been holdin' it for the admiral, but since you boys have this school project . . ."

"Hey, what luck!" cried Fat Albert to the sailor, who already must have been thinking of selling him the Liberty Bell.

While fantasies danced in our heads, the sailor reached into the booth and brought out a khaki packet about twice the size of a baseball card.

"That's *it*?" said Junior.

"Don't tell me you never seen none before," said the sailor.

"Oh, I seen tons, but mostly in cans."

"Man, Spanish Fly's a *powder.*"

"Of course it is. I musta been thinkin' about Spanish tuna."

"You boys know how to use this stuff? For your science project, I mean. You got some scientific girls that's gonna help you? 'Cause you don't do this project just with guys."

"Oh, we're definitely gonna use girls," said Harold.

"Okay, look, seein' that it's a school project, I'm not gonna charge ya for the stuff."

"Hey, thanks!" said Junior, and the rest of us echoed his gratitude. "Anytime we can do anything for *you* . . ."

The best thing we could have done for this sailor would have been to help him forget that we were some of the people he was protecting.

"Say, you boys wanna know what *happens* to the girls in this science project?" he said with a devilish smile. "I got a picture of a coupla students that tried it in the Philippines."

"That a Philadelphia school?" said Fat Albert.

The sailor laughed, again reached into the booth, and this time brought forth a photograph more remarkable than a shot of downtown Mars: a naked woman kissing a naked man.

"Spanish Fly made her do that?" said Fat Albert.

"Absolutely," said the sailor. "With her clothes on, that woman's a librarian."

For a few days after our educational trip to the Navy yard, Junior hid the magical packet in his closet, while we tried to arrange a party that the girls would never forget. I would've had it at my house, but I didn't want Russell there telling the girls that I didn't like anyone touching me.

At last, we chose Fat Albert's apartment, for we had convinced his mother that a party would help his social progress. Up till this point, his social progress had been that of a warthog and his mother was concerned.

"Yes, I'd like my Albert to meet some nice girls," she had said.

And he would, but not at this party, which had been planned to honor girls with a potential for depravity.

When Saturday came, I was as happy as if I'd just learned that Russell had been traded to another project. About an hour before the party was to begin, the four of us went to Fat Albert's apartment, not to help him fold napkins but to plan the best way to give the girls their little hormonal favors.

"How we gonna feed 'em powder?" said Harold, for that was what the sailor's packet contained.

"Easy, man," said Junior. "We just mix it in the punch."

"But punch is tough to do," said Eddie. "Easier just to sprinkle it on 'em. Pretend they got an itch or somethin'."

"No," said Junior, "it's gotta go *inside* 'em."

"An' when Fat Albert's mother drinks it," I said, "we better make sure his father's around."

"Hey, that was a good one, Cos," said Harold. "I think I get it."

"You sure it can go in the punch?" said Eddie to Junior.

"C'mon, I'll show ya."

And he led us to the bowl of punch, where he

poured some into a glass, dropped in a bit of the precious powder, and stirred it with two fingers, a sight to make any girl swear off liquids. But when his fingers came out, the Spanish Fly hadn't dissolved: it sat on the punch like newly fallen snow.

"A girl sees that," said Eddie, "she's gonna suspect somethin'."

"He's right," I said. "No girl's gonna drink powder unless she's really thirsty."

"Okay," said Junior, "then we sprinkle it on the cookies. It looks like sugar anyway."

"No it don't," said Fat Albert. "It looks like somethin' for fleas."

"So whadda we gonna do, Junior?" said Harold.

"Don't worry, I'll think of somethin'."

"You better," said Eddie, " 'cause there's just no point in a party unless the girls're takin' off their pants."

"My mother's not gonna be too crazy about it if she sees a lotta pants comin' off," said Fat Albert. "I mean, ones that ain't mine. So how we gonna do this, Junior?"

"Don't worry, I'll think of somethin'."

In spite of the challenge now facing us, I still was optimistic about what could happen at this party, even though the happening depended on that shaky thing called Junior's ability to think.

The girls began arriving at eight o'clock; and, as each one walked in, I wondered if she might be the potentially depraved girl of my dreams. These were the same old girls from all of our non-pharmaceutical parties, but now I saw them climbing the walls, and maybe even me. When the Ink Spots began to sing and the dancers began to square off in the center of the room, my mind was on a much less dreamy form of romance.

"So where's the stuff go, Junior?" said Eddie in a fierce whisper.

"It's gotta be the cookies," said our leader in lust. "Where are they?"

"They're still in the kitchen," said Fat Albert.

"Great! Get your mother outa there an' I'll dump the stuff on."

"How do I get her out? She loves it in there."

"Dance with her."

"That'll kill 'em," said Eddie with a grin. "Two tons o' dancin'."

"You gotta do it," Junior told Fat Albert. "I gotta be alone with the cookies."

And so, while the Ink Spots sang "Amor," Fat Albert danced with his mother and kept all eyes away from the kitchen, where Junior was turning the cookies into trips to the moon.

A few minutes later, we began offering them to the girls with casual desperation.

"Man, are these cookies *delicious*," I said to Elaine. "Have a few."

"No, thank you," she replied.

"Why not?"

"I gotta give you a reason?"

"Yeah, I wouldn't mind one," said 1950's Cookie Monster.

" 'Cause I'm not hungry, that's why."

"But dinner was two hours ago."

My style perhaps could have been smoother, but this, after all, was the first aphrodisiac I ever had pushed.

With a quizzical look, Elaine said, "Did you happen to *bake* these?"

"Well, I had a hand in 'em."

"Oh, that's sweet; I love it when boys bake things. Of course I'll try one."

Taking a cookie from my tray, she daintily bit off a piece—and then put down the rest.

"Gosh, William, I'm afraid I don't really like ginger. But it was lovely of you to bake them."

Damn Fat Albert's mother! Why did the stupid woman use *ginger*?

"Take one with a lotta sugar on it," I quickly said, "and you won't taste the ginger."

"Oh, I'm sure I still will."

"No you won't."

"William, what's wrong with you tonight?"

What was wrong with me? Just a sentimental desire to see Elaine chew her way out of her clothes.

In other parts of the room, my four restless co-conspirators also were having no luck with their sabotaged servings: the girls were eating the cookies, but they were remaining quietly dressed.

"It ain't *workin'*, Junior," said Harold as the five of us gathered in despair.

"It takes time."

"It'll happen when we ain't around."

"You think we can keep the party goin' another day?" I said.

But the party was short and depressingly sweet. Moreover, we never did learn what the aphrodisiac was, although Fat Albert's mother took a guess.

"I don' know," she said, "but these cookies kinda taste like cornstarch. I wonder if they'd be good for my feet."

11

Am I Insane?

In my first thirteen years as a man, I had kept finding memorable ways to fail at love: as a star-crossed crossing guard, as the refrigerated Romeo of the skating pond, and as the dreamy dispenser of Spanish Fly. All that, however, had been but rehearsal for real romance in the halls of Fitzsimons Junior High; for suddenly, the boyhood of buck-buck and the Booker monster gave way to a world that contained only a vision named Lori Newman.

After a few days in Fitzsimons, I was aware that a lot of the boys were singing a new song, a jazzy lyric that began,

There I go, there I go.
Pretty baby, you are the soul who snaps my control.

Such a funny thing,
But every time you're near me
I never can behave.
You give me a smile
And then I'm wrapped up in your magic . . .
Just let me get next to you.
Am I insane?

"Hey, man, what's the name of that song all you guys keep singin'?" I said one day to James Murray, the coolest boy in the whole ninth grade.

" 'Moody's Mood for Love,' " he replied. "It's the best way to get women."

"Well, that's how I want 'em: the best way. You know Lori Newman?"

"Yeah, a gas. In fact, the gas works."

"You think the song would work on her?"

"Is she female? It only works on women that's female."

He began to laugh, but I couldn't laugh too because the thought of conquering Lori Newman was making me feel the way I was supposed to feel in church.

"No kiddin'," I softly said.

"Bill, you ever had a woman?"

"Oh, sure—lots of 'em."

"Then you don't need the song."

"Well, I like to be safe. Can you teach it to me?"

"Check, Daddy. I got the record home."

And so, that day after school, I went to James's house, where he began to play "Moody's Mood for Love." He played it four or five times, while I sat there memorizing the words.

"Y' know, there's a party Saturday at Celia's," he finally said. "Everybody there'll know 'Moody's.' "

"Listen, James . . . here's the thing . . ."

"You ain't been invited."

"You could say that."

"I'll getcha in; Celia's got me playin' drums. And ol' Lori'll be there."

"Gee, James, that's *great*."

"No problem, Daddy. To glory with Lori, right?"

When I entered the party, Celia's phonograph already was playing The Song and I said to the first boy I saw, "Hey, my favorite song: 'A Moody Mood for Love.' "

" '*Moody's* Mood for Love,' " he replied.

"Right; I musta been thinkin' of that *other* one."

And suddenly, I saw Her, lighting up the far side of the room and laughing at something clearly unfunny that a tall boy beside her had just said. The days of Spanish Fly sandwiches were behind me now. I would have to win this beauty not with chemicals but my memory for music.

As I courageously cut across the floor, James began to accompany the song on his drums and the rhythm so possessed me that I found myself bopping toward Lori while also singing along. If her taste in men was for one from Looney Tunes, she would be mine.

At last, I reached her and I stopped my bop and my song. It was time to be conventionally alluring.

"Hey, Lori," I said, once again letting my mouth lead my mind by a considerable distance, "whatcha doin'?"

"She's waitin' for a trolley," said the tall boy and Lori laughed.

Battling back, I quickly said, "Don't you really dig 'Moody's in the Mood for Love'?"

"Yes," she replied, and her speaking to me filled me with hope.

"Wanna dance?"

"Okay."

Okay! What poetry! And she had said it to *me!*

Nervously, I put my arm around her and began to lead her in a—something. Was "Moody's Mood for Love" a fox trot, rhumba, or waltz? The answer, of course, was irrelevant because I didn't know any of them; I was still trying to master the march. Whatever it might have been, "Moody's" was a dance for only the fastest feet. I was fast, but between sewers—with a football, not a girl, in my arms.

Nevertheless, I felt such desire to win this prize that I did something bold to hang on to the beat.

"Hey," I said, "you wanna lead?"

"The boy is supposed to lead," she replied.

"Yeah, but I thought I'd give you a crack at it; I really like you. Listen, Lori . . . before we dance—no matter who's in charge—I gotta ask ya somethin'."

"Yes?" she replied.

"You think . . . you think somebody's gotta be a special age to be in love?"

"Well, over eleven, I guess."

I now was two *years* over eleven, so this rapture was overdue. And it needed no Spanish Fly, that magic dust for athlete's foot that I had tried to use in a recent rite of passage at Fat Albert's, a rite with none of the romance that now was turning me dizzier than usual.

"Listen . . . d' ya happen to be goin' steady right now?" I said.

"We barely know each other, Bill. You have to get to *know* somebody."

"Oh, we could certainly do that too. So you'll think about it, right? I don't need an answer right away. I'm not askin' other people."

"Why don't we just dance? I'll lead."

"Hey, thanks. You think anybody'll know? I mean, it's hard to tell who's doin' the pushin', right? You hafta know geometry."

"You're a funny boy," she said with a smile, "but you've got a good mind."

"A good mind to what?"

"Let's dance."

As I led her out to the floor so that she could start leading me, I could clearly hear, above the music, manhood calling to me:

Buck-buck number one, come in.

Epilogue

///

To Tell the Truth

What is the essence of childhood? I discovered it a few years ago when my youngest daughter, Evin, who had been home with chicken pox for a week, received a packet of letters from her second-grade classmates, one of which was unforgettable:

> *Dear Evin:*
> *I hope you get well soon.*
> *Mr. Dickey forced us to write this letter. So I'm not writing it because I like you.*
>
> *Your friend,*
> *Leon*

There, in that qualified get-well wish, is the shining simplicity and eloquent candor that could only have come from a child. Innocent of all guile, Leon told Evin that she was getting shotgun sympathy.

"Sort of a funny letter from Leon, don't you think?" I said to Evin after we had read his fundamental indifference to the state of her health.

"Oh, Dad," she said, "Leon's just a boy and you know how boys are."

"No, how are they?"

"Stupid."

"But I'm a boy."

"Well, don't go around reminding people."

"So you think girls are better than boys."

"Dad, everyone knows they are. Mr. Dickey couldn't force the *girls* who hate me to hope I get well. You'll notice there's nothing from Jessica. She's wished on me worse than the chicken pox."

That innocence, that honesty, that logic—they are childhood. They are the Fountain of Youth for which Ponce de León was searching. Another Leon who was just another dopey boy.